LANDSCAPING FOR BEGINNERS

A Step-by-step guide to DIY landscaping as a professional gardener. Enhance your garden and improve the value of your house with stones, perennials and annuals plants.

By

Roger Miller

Contents

Introduction

Many people dream of having the most amazing front or back yard, the most comfortable place of the town, where entertaining space to dazzle their friends and social get-togethers but have absolutely no idea of where to begin. Most start with small-scale DIY projects such as flowers around the front porch, a little mulch around the trees, or even a small raised garden with a few herbs. That is certainly sensible, but time-consuming: it could take years to get to the place that you have envisioned! Some get somewhat of a design based on what they see around them, maybe keeping up with theirneighbors. Everyone tries to have the greatest garden to get the neighbors talking and get their admiration so vehemently desire. Hence, they immediately go into massive debt to get there. Whatever the case may be, if you want to improve your house value and have the most beautiful and tidy garden in your neighborhood, without spending too much time and money, landscaping is all you need.

Many people think gardening is only "having cure about the plants", but it is more than this. **Landscaping, specifically, is a type of gardening that includes changing and improving the garden design and consequently its value.**

How can people improve their garden value? Simple! By landscaping, people can create specific areas that meet their family' need and understand how to maintain their garden during the seasons.

Becoming a landscaper allows you to transform your design garden project into reality!

Whatever the condition is your garden now, whichever situation you are in, is enough a motivation to create something beautiful. Thanks to this book, you will learn how to create your project step by step and analyze your garden to understand its current situation and evaluate if you can or cannot make a specific area in it. Landscapes can be complex and time-demanding to build, but with the right source of information, techniques and ideas, anyone can master the art of landscaping.

Like if you want to achieve a goal, you need to have a game plan; therefore, you need to develop your timeline to make things smooth. The best way to start is to draw a map, not a typical map, but more of a timeline. Take a look at your garden situation and write all aspects in a paper. A landscape comprises living as well as non-living objects, usually gardens/plant decorations, even which around your house, and everything will have to be included in your landscape project. Look at catalogs, the internet, local home improvement stores, and find the elements you would like to have and add those, writing even their price. Take pictures of elements you like, things you see while you're out and save pictures you see online. Don't make impulse buys; don't fall for some item that any seller wants to stick you, only because it is low-price, when it comes to improving your home. **Your home is your castle; treat it as such.** Ensure you can see your project since its beginning; this will help you make the best decisions and come to the ultimate conclusion. Once you have finished a game plan, make your budget plan, and establish exactly the budget and the steps you want to do chronologically. You could find a contractor; however, by this guide you will be able to realize all your project yourself!

Do you think there are too many aspects to look at? Don't worry; I will guide you step by step, from the beginning to the finish, providing you detailed and precise information about how a landscape should be built, what features or materials to use, how to set a budget, and all you must know to realize your awesome landscaping project. **So, let's go!**

Chapter 1: What is Landscaping

By nature, landscaping is the design of public and outdoor landscapes to meet particular specifications or objectives. For example, in a public park, these goals may involve the landscaping of an area to include park user seating, lighting, and a playground for young ones. Landscape gardening is also referred to as landscape architecture, which is even a more descriptive term because landscape gardeners usually design, prepare, construct and supervise the construction of a landscape area on which they were hired to work. Landscapers also provide many extra services due to the work's nature, which may include building, carpentry, tree surgery, fencing, and groundwork. The landscaping history stems from designing, planning, and managing large estates, manors, royal palaces, and residences. During the 18th and 19th centuries, the demand for ever more lavish and decadent gardens between the royal palaces and noble residences grew. Thanks to these commissions, we can now enjoy such delights as the Palace of Versailles Gardens in France, designed by the famous André Le Nôtre, and the magnificent Palace Gardens of Blenheim in Oxford shire, UK. All through the 19th century, the need for urban planning grew, with many towns' rapid development and growth. The term 'landscape architect' was first used by professionals when Frederick Law Olmsted adopted the term in 1863. Olmsted was, in fact, responsible for establishing many early practices in American landscape architecture in some of his great works, including the iconic Central Park in New York City. Our main concern is to develop our yards or companies since we all admire the beauty. We put flowering plants here and there, fences that serve as boundaries, table and chairs for having meals or refreshments outdoors, swings, garden gnomes, and other material items we want to have on our lawns. Such and other practices are collectively called landscaping, which presupposes a specific area to be built. Most homeowners choose a garden in the landscape. What is landscape gardening? As its name suggests, it's a sort of landscape that turns an area into a garden.

Gardening is essentially a process design making using living elements, especially plants, both flowering and non-flowering plants. Garden owners can do this, but others are hiring professional landscapers to develop their gardens. Professional landscapers have trained the basic gardening principles, and others may take short courses for that. On the other hand, while spending time working at their own gardens, garden owners attain good experiences. Other people have made this a hobby, particularly women, while others make it an expansion of their imagination. Everyone can do gardening, regardless of its job, its house's condition, or its time available. Knowing what landscape gardening is as a whole will result in the successful creation of a garden that meets the landowner's goal, needs, or desires. The gardening, meanwhile, is notjust about the designs and layouts. It is also about how it would be maintained after it has been put up after all the dynamic landscape gardening is. Working with it continues as long as there are tendentious plants and flowers and structures to preserve. You can add or remove structures, you can renovate them, you can plant other flowers or trees, or you can do anything to improve your garden continually. Other gardeners would even develop one section at a time, occasionally putting more materials and plants into each section.

Basic principles of landscaping

A landscape includes whether non-living components and animals, and all of these should be considered in your project. Some examples of non-living things can be water, rocks, soil, gravel roads, timber, water beds, flower beds, fire pit, benches, fence, furniture; these are called "landscape components". The plants and the animals inhabiting the area serve as the fine exemplar for the living components. The way these components are selected and coordinated together serve as the contrast between how a landscape may look: good or bad. Landscaping is divided into two parts; **soft landscaping** and **hard landscaping**; the first includes all the vegetable living features as plants, trees and shrubs. On the other hand, hard landscaping includes non-living and hard surfaces such as pathways, walkways, entry walks, ponds, streams, statues, sculptures, etc. To understand the art of landscaping very well, you have to know its "rules".

The basic principles of landscaping consist of seven main components:

Unity

Unity in landscape compromises consistency, quality and repetition of the design. Repetition is used to bring your design together by repeating such elements that contain plants and landscape decoration. Unity is attained through grouping, positioning, or arrangement of several individual components that emanates a sense of similarity, creating a common theme. An example of this perhaps is using the same plants instead of a range of plants of different color, shape, size, and texture. The same structural components may also be another exemplar. Using many different plants or objects may create a chaotic and not very pleasing atmosphere in the landscape. To create unity in this landscape design, the same color continuation; texture, shape, size and proximity of plants are used.

Balance

In simple terms, balance is a way of achieving equilibrium; equality. The two balances are symmetrical and asymmetrical balance. As the two sides of the landscape are homogenous in symmetrical balance, asymmetrical may agree to differ. In asymmetrical balance, each half is divergent but has similar visual-imaginary weight. Symmetry is of most importance in formal landscape designs.

Symmetrical and Asymmetrical balance

In symmetrical balance identical decorations, plants, and textures, structural components_keep the unity in the place. In contrast, in asymmetrical balance a lot of the same plants and textures, structural components are used for the sake of unity; nevertheless, each side differ, making the asymmetry more relaxed while keeping it in order.

Contrast and harmony

Contrast helps emphasizing some aspects of architectural-landscape design, and harmony helps unify aspects of the landscape arrangement. The contrast between the components attracts the attention of the viewer when placed side by side. The collocation of all art elements or vibrant colors is used to accomplish harmony and contrast of the landscape overall. The contrast, in contradiction to harmony, must not be exaggerated. Usually, contrasts are used to enhance a feature's attractiveness that passer-by may find pleasing. Some examples are contrasting leaf texture, color or shape and light garden furniture, painted walls and fences that enhance the landscape's beauty. Contrast is not only limited to the plants. Other non-living components can also be of use.

Color

Color gives the element of vibrancy to your landscape pattern and style. Warm, hot colors seem to move towards you, in a way demanding more of your attention (i.e., red, orange, yellow), making the object look nigh.

While cool colors such as green, blue, white, silver, etc. appear to be moving away, giving a more relaxing aura to the landscape garden.

Each season has its colors:

- ***Winter*** has a bright yellow color.
- ***Spring*** has a purple and pink color.
- ***Summer*** has blue, red and white color.
- ***Autumn*** has a bronze and red color.

You can create a beautiful effect using complementary colors, for example:

- The yellow and blue flowers in the same place to create a brilliant contrast.
- A red shrub (as a Photinia) on a green lawn.
- Red Flowers and plants that match the black of the rocks in your garden.

Line

Lines are of the most important in a landscape, one might like to call them the mother of all. Lines have been made of use to convey a deep and remote illusion, to highlight an object, influence motion, or focus attention to one specific area or also known as a focal point. The flower bed, edge of a sidewalk, outline of a building, walkways, fire pit, may serve as a fine exemplar.

Proportion

The size of one element with respect to the other is proportion. This needs some preparation and thought among all the other landscape principles. All landscape elements must be adequately balanced. The size and scaling of the components must be in proper proportion in terms of the landscape as a whole. For example, large trees or plants may not be proportionate in a small lawn, large furniture in a small space may be awkward from a visual perspective, and a large statue on a small plant may make the plant itself go unnoticed. If done correctly, the proportion can change the overall atmosphere or aura of the landscape to either a dull one or a vibrant one.

Transition

The transformation in landscape design indicates the scale and varying plant and color intensity as a gradual change in transition. Color, texture, form, tone, and space are also various forms of transition. The form is the contour of three-dimensional objects. The extent to which forms are solid is known as mass. The impact of lighter, thicker, or leaves that are darker in color provides the landscape with an enhanced mass. (Plants have varied masses; some might be denser while some are open). When defining space, the volume determined by the boundaries of plants, trees, bushes or shrubs, sky, ground area, and the outer layer of leaves of a group of plants or trees is used (canopy) or hence is space itself. Texture alludes to the components of landscape design: rough or fine, raw or smooth. The texture is necessary when looking at the size, especially in smaller, more intimate areas. Many different textures are in the wood, gravel, stones, plants, and also water. Tone serves as the connection between the texture, color, and light of a landscape's components. Different tones change the landscape's overall look, so one must choose the right tones and colors when designing. As said above, color is the correlation between contrast and harmony, the use of cool and warm colors may make a big difference to the landscape.

Why do Landscape gardening?

1) Environmental Benefits

Grass, rather than cement and asphalt, is much cooler; it functions as an "air conditioner" for the nearby area. Moreover, lawns tend to be 31 degrees cooler than the asphalt, and it's 20 degrees cooler as compared to bare soil.

Trees that shade homes can decrease temperature up to 40 degrees.

Grass plays an important role in removing and capturing dust, particles of smoke, and any other pollutants there might be; it also produces oxygen. Healthy and well-maintained lawns absorb toxic runoff that may potentially be filtered into water bodies, while grasses absorb and break down carbon dioxide into oxygen. Typically, a 50'x50' lawn typically supplies a family with four members with an ample amount of oxygen!

Plants and lawns significantly decrease noise pollution; as compared to hard surfaces like concrete and paving, they can decrease the noise by 20 to 30%. Turfgrass delays and soaks up runoff into water bodies. Then, it is essential that landscapes and lawns continue to exist as a viable part of well-maintained communities, particularly in those areas where water is restricted and has drought problems. There are quite a few techniques that can help manage landscapes and lawns to limit water demand and still provide significant environmental benefits.

2) Physical and Psychological Benefits

There are detailed research and data on human contact effects with trees, plants, and grass. Studies have found that people experience emotional relief and relaxation by communicating with nature and simply viewing it. Harvard Health Publications says children that have ADHD tend to have a greater concentration after visiting outdoors. Workers work more efficiently, and their cognitive function is also increased when employed in environments whit a lot of greenery; but the most important factor is what people instinctively experience and feel about plants and greenery in their lives – that if it enhances their life's quality and comfort if they want to make an effort to better their lifestyles.

3) Get the Admiration of the Neighbors

How would you feel if your neighbors congratulate you for your garden beauty? Receiving appreciation makes everyone happy! To have the coolest garden in the neighborhood isn't a life challenge, but it is definitely something will make you proud!

4) More Security for Your Home and Your Family

In a clean and tidy garden, you can live better. If one garden is dirty, messy, and there are broken items, fences, or paving, people could fall or get hurt. Fortunately, landscaping art can solve all of these problems. By creating a logical landscape, repairing the fences, and replacing the broken paving, your life quality will improve a lot! Kids could be run on your lawn without risks, and older adults could be walking on the pathway and sit down on a bench without it cracking!

Another aspect of landscaping is the improvement of your home security in general: putting tall fences or hedges could prevent thieves from entering.

Following, there are some plants you could add to your garden border to protect your home better:

- You can put some tall ornamental grasses on your borders; three of the best are **maiden grass, bamboo,** and **zebra grass** that they are low-maintenance. However, some bamboo types are invasive a lot, so keep in mind informing you very before buying and planting it.

- If you are not a fan of fences, a tall hedge can do for you. If you opt for a formal garden design, you can prune hedges following the style or topiary. However, keep in mind that maintaining hedges could be a lot of work.
- In addition to shrubs and ornamental grasses, another beautiful choice in landscaping could be evergreen trees. If you live in a windy area, they will offer privacy and also form windbreaks. Put a hedge of holly shrubs could keep thieves off your property, because its barbed leaves are not exactly comfortable to brush up against. This should keep most of burglars out, except the most determined.

Chapter 2: How do I start landscaping?

Let's start with the design approach. When you're finally starting to design your landscape, you have to think of an approach. It is necessary to observe the area first and put your plans together because if you don't take the necessary steps to the beginning, the whole design will be ruined. The next step is to carefully observe all the elemental components and features in the area and consider including them in your final design. For example, if there are rocks included in the landscape, you might use them and create the desired design. Remember that you're looking for the most efficient way to reach the design you have thought about. You also need to ensure that the already present features and structures will suit your new landscape design. And be thoughtful if the area you're designing can afford your desired changes and designs. The most important thing is the 'end look.' For example, every person would want their home landscape to look pleasing to the eye and solve some practical problems, such as poor drainage. So, keep everything in mind and go through with a proper and thorough design plan. Here are some questions you can ask yourself before working on the area:

- What is the scope of the design?
- How do you deal with the existing features and structures on the landscape?
- About the design you have considered; does it fit the landscape and its structures?
- Is there enough space and room for the design you are considering?
- Will the design you're considering make the area look more pleasing?

Steps to create your project on paper sheet

1) Identification of area/landscape lines

This step can be made quite easier if you get the map, which shows you area lines and the house's location on the area or property. The map could be of any kind; a plat, architect's or builder's plan, etc. I suggest you take the house planimetry. The map could include the hardscapes and structures that are fixed; houses, exits, entryways, walkways, walls, driveways, and so on. Although it mostly depends on where you live, these papers can be obtained with ease with papers that you acquired when you bought your home. If the area lines are difficult to verify, you may have to consult a licensed cartographer to verify the area's boundaries for your land to test them. The survey plan could also be used as a foundation for the layout that you would be making use of in further steps.

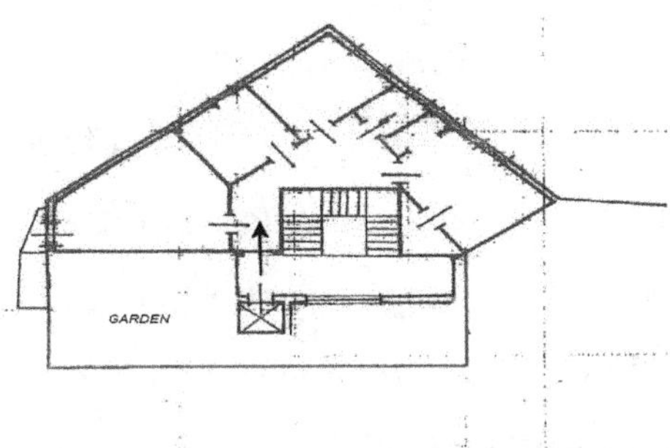

Use a paper for tracing to create a rough drawing of your area/property to develop your base/plot plan. If your land property is huge, you might want to split the design into multiple sketches or drawings; landscape areas in front, areas in side-view, areas in the backyard, or you could just use a bigger paper. Your scaled drawing should nevertheless show you the typical shape of the area or property. Make sure you mark the road and lines of the property. It is useful to have an arrow to pinpoint the direction of the north.

2) Selecting equipment

Collect the necessary equipment to record sizes: 50 to 100 ft accurately. Tape scale, erasers, pencils, etc. and a huge clipboard clasping the tracing paper. You can also use measuring paper if that is more convenient for you instead of tape scale-measure. You should also have a scale for drawing and a graph paper for converting your rough drawing to a scaled one. It will be convenient if you have another partner to take measurements when using a tape measure. If the help is not available, use a screwdriver to assist you in holding the tape in place when you measure.

3) Final base plan

Use the graph paper to draw the final plan using the biggest scale that fits your property area. For instance, 100 foot by 70 foot will adjust correctly on a 10 x 10 sq. inch graph paper x 8 1⁄2 x 11 piece, when 1"= 10 feet scale is used. Graph paper is available at book shops and sections of the office that supply the stores. Create the final plan (base plan) by drawing a line along the grid center to show your road's edge and streets in front of the house. Another line should be drawn to portray the street on the side if you have many corners. Then mark the direction of your compass on the final plan with an arrow indicating the north. Put east, west, and south in the relevant area. All restrictions, facilities, and right of ways should be found that are connected with your area or property. Most cities have sidewalks located on the city area or property, and the property line sometimes begins in the sidewalk or near it. Avoid planting on areas mostly used for street expansion such as easement area. Pinpoint the line of the front of the property after distance to the easement is determined and gently draw on the paper you're using. Sketch the side and boundaries at the back after that. In case the boundaries at the side do not seem to be parallel, then the boundary line at the front should be drawn. After that, by the usage of the sightline, the back-boundary line can be drawn. By doing this, side boundary or boundary at the side can then be pinpointed. These four boundary lines are necessary to draw for a correct outline of the property, so be careful. You can now sketch in your house by pinpointing the corner you previously measured for your rough drawing. It will have a certain distance from the closest property line and the street/road. Find the corner from the graph paper by counting the squares. Then draw your home's measurements and shape. Make sure you pointed out the widths and heights of the windows, doors, and windowsill height from ground level.

For the next step, shift all the features, including those that will impact your landscape design in your rough drawing or sketch, for drawing the curved feature, onto the final plan. Shift all the dot measurements with the area, including a curved edge from the tracing paper to scaled drawing. Approximate the curved line by using a French curve. You can get a French curve from office supply shops. By rotating the French curve, have at least three points touched, which you have pinpointed by the curve's outer and inner edge. This curve line does an accurate representation of your feature.

After you're done adding all the components and features, your property's base plan will be quite precise and correct. But if you fail to add all the features in one base plan, you can always create another one, like an inventory sheet. If the base plan is created on the tracing paper, it could be quite convenient as you can place it over the base plan for a finalized drawing of your property. This finished base plan will serve as your go-to map when you're finally creating your landscape.

4) Site analysis

Site analysis is an important and necessary step to take. For example, analyzing the conditions of plants, soil, and the overall area is important for further modifications and improvements you want to make to the landscape to enhance the beauty and make the utmost use of nature's beauty. Take a new sheet or piece of tracing paper and put it over the base plan. Trace 'all' the features and components of the base plan. This second copy will serve as your site analysis map and help you further your site advancements.

The next paragraphs will help you monitor sun characteristics and patterns accurately, shade, water, noise, soils, the shape of the property, drainage of surfaces, and scenery. Mark all the estimated whereabouts of every item and thing and their conditions. Make use of arrows to specify the views, slopes, etc. Have a look at what you have built up till now. It should probably look like your property now. See the spaces and the correlation between them. Is the area where you usually park too close to the door you mostly use? You might notice that some areas are incompatible with being used simultaneously. Is the view from your living room's window the piles of wood and tools your neighbor has been hoarding for quite a while? Let's hope that's not the case. To avoid such views and inconvenience, you must mark and specify all the areas included in your landscape. A precise and detailed site analysis will do wonders when you progress to further design steps.

If in your garden there are architectural features, like windows or ancient brick wall, ask yourself if you want to remove them or not. If you don't want to remove them, first of all, analyze their conservation state, then identify which modifications you want to make to them. You should consider very well what types of shrubs or trees you want to plant close to the architectural features to highlight their beauty. For example, if you have a decorated window that is high 2ft above the ground, you should put plants high 2ft maximum below the window to allow people to look at its beauty.

5) Understanding the features of the environment

The sun's movement throughout the days and seasons is an important thing to note for developing shaded and open areas. Also, do not forget the movements of the sun during winters. Specify with arrows howthe winter sun affects your home so that you could have suitable shaded areas for summers and open areas for winters where sunlight can reach and keep the area warm during winters.

Winds are another important factor to consider as they can be harsh when the weather is not so good. Note the wind's overall orientation and place screens in places where the direction of prevailing winds is to protect you from bad weather. State the areas that are most impacted by the surrounding noises on your analysis sheet/plan. Noises from neighborhood, nearby subways, can really impact your quality time for relaxing. One way to avoid noise is to place shrubs and trees. They help in minimizing the noises to an extent.

Another main factor to consider is the kind of soil you're using as your foundation. It can significantly affect the conditions of your foliage and grass lawns. Look at the soil around your house. A soil or a ground test should be carried out every 20 feet on the sides. Avoid collecting mortar or cement chips as it could destroy your plants. Remember to remove these substances before you prepare the soil. If you do not know how to take a sample and submit it, try to contact the extension office for help. They will provide you with a sheet full of instructions and also sample boxes of soil, which can help.

Surface drainage should be included in your analysis sheet. Make a note of how and where your water flows out of your property and into the property; are there other areas where water is flooding into your property? Take a note of the area where water is continuously standing for quite an extended period. And importantly, do add the areas where eroding is happening. The best way to mark your observations is during multiple rainfall occasions. The site analysis should determine the visibility of views seen from all the directions from within your house and your property.

Specify these on the notes of your analysis. Take a look at the checklist before you proceed to the next step:

- □ Look at the movement and patterns of the sun during all the seasons;
- □ Identify all water drainage system; spigots, pipes, areas where water usually drains, downspouts…
- □ Identify areas where the surface is lower than level-ground; water usually stagnates there, eroding the surface;
- □ Identify all of the existing trees, ponds, rocks, structures, you won't remove from your garden;
- □ Identify which areas are the quietest and which are not (maybe too close to the road); you could install the screens to reduce noises;
- □ Identify areas where the wind usually blows stronger and which ones are more protected;
- □ Look at the currently materials and colors of your house;
- □ Identify the sites in which there are windows or other architectural features;
- □ Identify the warmest areas, the coldest ones, and areas where shade is already present;
- □ Identify areas where are present slopes, hills, knolls, differences in height;
- □ Look at all the views from the property; the best and the worst;
- □ Check the current conditions of all the trees plants, shrubs, flowers, etc.
- □ Check all structures that need to be fixed or improved (patios, fences, furniture, etc.);
- □ Look for eventual toxic, harmful or diseased plants, and cure or remove them;
- □ Make a careful assessment of the fauna near your garden and decide whether to create a small habitat reserve.

6) Consider the wants and needs of your family

With a thorough and comprehensive plan of the site, you're prepared to list your expected areas for use now. The needs of every family member may differ, for example, activities done outdoors.

Followings are the type of places that you might want to consider adding in your landscape:

- Areas for your pet's, example stalls or a big lawn
- Entertainment zones
- The area where you could sit and have a nice sunbath, read books
- A swimming pool for water activities
- A little storage room for tools or any kind of equipment
- Sidewalks, gardens, paths
- Any kind of water feature
- Areas you might want to do some cooking, for example, an outdoor barbeque party
- A small lounge for a sitting area

Chapter 3: Landscape materials guide

Drainage Channels

Drainages are very important in a garden; they allow to drain the water excess, avoiding flooding. They are fundamentals for draining large areas of paving and ramps or paths contained between walls. To ensure this, make sure the downspouts and gutters are draining to the outside of the bed. This will allow the rainwater to wash your dirt, plants, and mulch. If you don't know where you have downspouts, then wait for it to rain; then look at the ground to see where the water drains off the roof and this could be an area in which you pave with large-sized gravel or rocks, because these will help flow the water out the area. You should avoid planting in these areas because will remain too much water. The width of the channel must be related to the size of the gully; channels can also be built alongside roads and driveways, offering an interesting design solution.

Types of Channels

Channels can be dished or flat and can be made of variety of materials. Dished channels are usually of pre-cast concrete or stone, the latter are expensive. Flat channels should have the surface sufficiently shaped to ensure the flow of water to the drainage gully. An alternative to the surface channels is using a “stat curb” section or a glazed half round channel with a cast iron grating. Both types need a high degree of maintenance to prevent silting up.

Tree Surrounds

If trees are incorporated in paved areas, a soil pocket is required around each trunk, and an adequate surface water supply must be able to pass through the soil to the tree roots. If the earth around the tree area is sealed, the tree may dry up and die due to lack of water and air. Another important point is that sufficient space is left to allow for the tree’s natural growth, including the trunk's expansion.

Choice of Surrounds

There are several methods of detailing the tree surrounds: a radial-paving pattern of precut concrete units with drainage holes can be used, or bricks can be laid around the tree to a radius of approximately 1.5-2.0m. Tree grids or grills in concrete or cast iron can be obtained from various manufacturers; one of the edgings described can retain the paving outside the tree surround, infilled with granular material such as cobblestones or gravel. A curb is sometimes misguidedly fitted around a tree to protect it and to edge the paving. This should not be done. It breaks up the horizontal surface and forms a useless miniature flowerbed for creating litter, while offering only negligible protection to the tree trunk. It could also cause accidents in a heavily used pedestrian area.

EDGING: One of easiest ways to achieve a specific gardening effect for the landscape is to create or decorate border edgings. You can use concrete, plastic, aluminum, brick boundaries, to create edges in your landscape gardening project. Choose if you want to use only one type or mix and match. When working around existing trees, you should choose an edging that will not damage any roots close to the surface. Edgings are usually flush with the surrounding paving to enable the surface run-off to drain into the tree surround.

Infill Material

This should be porous so that the surface run-off can water the trees. The material should be lightly compacted by hand. If there are existing trees, the soil should not be dug all around the tree, and the infill material should be placed on the hand-compacted topsoil. If you have pergolas with various creepers to feel semi-enclosed spaces, you could make a partial variation: you should use screens to break up spaces further. Perforated stone or latticed screen, usually with an ornamental pattern is used as screens to create vertical patterns.

Pavements

The base plane surface is often the natural surface of the earth. Its structure consists of various soil layers, ranging from thin to deep, and can sometimes be covered with vegetation. The general composition of the earth plane is mineral: its component could range in hardness from diamond through solid granite, limestone, shales of clay, sands, and loams. The supporting strength, stability of the soil and mineral strata depends not only on each stratum's nature, but also on its angle of inclination, water, relation to the other strata and the surface. The base plane is closely related to the site structure or site project diagram, with its studied arrangement of use areas; for this is the plane on which we are most concerned with use. When we look at a project plan, we always see it laid out on a ground plan. The shapes, materials and texture imposed here are best suited to the proposed use and coordinate them into a cohesive plan.

If the base plane is improperly developed, nothing that follows has meaning. Here we establish the type of use of each area and the surface it should have, the starting plans, the objectives, and each user's relationship with all the others. If we leave something out here, our plan could be a fail, no matter how well contrived the rest of the spatial enclosure.

The treatment of the base plane is important to the accomplishment of proper transitions. If well-handled, the shapes and patterns of the base may subtly or powerfully relate a structural element to the site. Through the treatment of the ground surfaces, we may relate our structural element to the other. We may accentuate, articulate, and coordinate, by contrast or harmony, all elements placed on base surfaces, through the treatment of their design. In other cases, the paved area may be neither a background nor a path, but rather a pattern, sufficient in itself, nor at least which plays the role of a beautiful carpet to the surrounding walls of the buildings or hedges.

Selection of Paving Materials

It depends on different factors:

- Cost and availability
- Durability
- Freedom from cracking
- Another failure
- Appearance
- Texture range
- Color
- Safety, noise, light reflectivity
- Non glare

Some of the major materials used for the pavement are given below:

- Concrete
- Cobbles
- Bricks
- Slate
- Gravel or Pebbles
- Granite
- Tiles
- Natural Stones

Due to it is mineral, in fact, and in connotation, the earth plane suggests the use of those materials that are mineral or of mineral extraction. The soil and the moisture and the frost it retains our powerful erodes and corroders. From the structural point of view, extreme care must be taken in the selection of materials like rock, gravel, water, sand and asphalt, ceramics, tile, such materials seem compatible.

Sand set brick paving could be slippery but is very elegant; the concrete path is the simplest to install and is also elegant. Steppingstone and Flagstone walkways are both the most common paving styles: although they are very affordable, they are easy to install and match with many designs. If you are going to install swimming pool or Spa area, I suggest installing wood paving, to create a more relaxing atmosphere.

Pedestrian Paving

When choosing the material, it is preferable to reflect the local vernacular as this does not create a sense of place. The separation of pedestrian from vehicular surfacing provides an opportunity to create a far more interesting design. It is necessary to provide for pedestrians as well as vehicles: a mixture of materials can be used, or the same material, in a different color can be used for vehicles, but with the increasing appropriate foundation thickness. To ensure that any surface paving material retains its final laid position, especially sub-grade and base, both the ground and under materials must be prepared thoroughly. Paving usually has a base and sub-grade underneath, and both of these must be compacted thoroughly. The sub-grade should be well compacted either by hand or by mechanical means. The required contour of the paving is obtained by shaping the sub-grade. The base is usually of hard-core, compacted by a 3-ton roller or a 500kg vibrating roller.

Technical elements in paving

Joints: tight, unfilled joints are only possible with units of regular size and shape such as precast concrete paving flags or precast concrete interlocking paving with which tight jointing is usual. Joint between paving brick, stone setts and natural paving are best filled with a 1:3 cement mortar or a 1:4 lime mortar. The mortar is brushed dry into the joints and then watered. This method reduces risk of mortar staining the paving. If plant or moss growth in the joint is to be encouraged, the joints can be filled with sifted topsoil or sand mixed with bone metal.

Edges: a rigid edge must contain flexible pavements; either a precast concrete edging with a concrete surround or a timber edging held by timber pages. Small rigid units should be contained by a row of units, need no edging when adjoined by turfed or flexible paved area, where concrete strips should be provided under the paving to prevent the base falling away.

Falls: the gradient of the fall required to clear surface water varies according to the nature of the surface. Recommended falls are; concrete 1:60; brick paving 1:60; bituminous surface 1:40; paving slab 1:70; gravel 1:30; public pavements 1:50.

Kerbs

Kerbs are necessary to control the lateral spread of the road, control surface water drainage from the road and to discourage vehicles' encroachment onto footpaths and grass verges. In certain situations, edging its roads with upstanding kerbs could spoil an area's character, and they can be dangerous where fast-moving traffic is prevalent; in such circumstances, slush kerbs (usually of 125-250 mm pre-cast concrete) are used. There is no reason why other material or design approaches should not be considered. Any road kerb detail will have to be agreed with the adopting authority.

Setting Kerbs

Kerbs should be laid before the base and surfacing of the road is usually laid on 100-150 mm bed of concrete (dry mix of 1:3:6). The concrete should be well haunted at the back of the kerb. Joints should be formed with cement and sand mortar (1:3). Expansion joints in kerbs to flexible roads should be at 20m. With concrete roads the joints should coincide with the joints in the road slab. Filler should be placed between the kerb as between the road slabs.

Walls

Natural stone or slate used in the garden for walls, paths and driveways, will beat beauty and mellowness. By natural stone, or slate, I mean suitable hill and mountain stone, or slate, that may be found in your region. If the stone or slate in your area looks good and is easy enough to work, will do the job you have in mind; it could be logical to use it rather than import stone or slate needlessly from interstate or, for that matter, from abroad. Not only, possibly, will the imported stone or slate be expensive, but it may look out of place (or, of course, it may not, but I always prefer to use local materials where possible).

Wall construction

About wall construction, the foundations on which the brick, then stone or slate, rests must be deep enough and wide enough to take the weight of the materials without moving or cracking: a wall foundation that is too narrow may cause the wall to tilt, and also its fall!

Wall foundation depths can vary depending on the type of soil and temperature. For example, clay soil could shrink and crack in dry conditions. Wall foundations in very cold areas have to be down below frost lift. If any action lifts the wall, the chances of it cracking will be great. Therefore, ascertain your soil and soil temperature, and build your foundations accordingly. I will explain how to create a wall and its foundations later in this book; however, you can get all of the information about this topic from a suitable state advisory service, if you need it. **You could easily build a small garden wall, say up to one meter tall, provided you are fit enough; however, I suggest you call an expert to build high garden walls (higher than 1 meter).** If you intend doing so, however, I strongly advise that you get in a fair amount of practice well before building your wall in the garden because there is nothing so ugly (and possibly dangerous) as a wall that is badly laid, especially if it facing the road for all to see. Pay attention to this book's information, and, if you need, call an expert or take a part-time further education course on bricklaying, on working in stone or slate. As they say, practice makes perfect, and people have been known to select a suitable firm area, such as a concrete floor, and practice bricklaying. If you have a wall you tear down in your garden, remember that the walls must take down before the mortar has set, and the floor and bricks are cleaned of mortar before you dug foundations for another wall. The bricks from the older wall can still be used, but the mortar is no longer suitable for building walls and discarded.

Mortar

The correct mortar constituents for brickwork, stonework or slate work joints is vital. The mortar used for brickwork may be very different from that used for stonework or slate work. The right proportions of suitable sand, cement and lime is critical, as this will reduce the incidence of cracking. Today, there is a tendency to use a mortar plasticizer with the sand and cement, that gives a similar plasticity to that of lime.

Foundation Thickness

Usually, a small garden wall's concrete foundation is a minimum of 150 mm deep, and suitably wider than the brick, stone or slate wall to allow for pressure. The thickness will depend on the wall's load, and may be from 150 to 300 mm. I repeat, it is important to have the correct foundations to help protect the wall from breaking should the soil move. You must use the correct mix of concrete laid down by the building regulations that exist in your local zone, applicable to building garden walls. If it should be necessary to use any concrete reinforcing rods to help strengthen it, a professional foundation builder should be contacted.

Brickwork Bonds for Walls

By studying books on bricklaying, you will see that there are many brickwork bond styles for walls. Be aware that the various names of brick bonds are not universal (e.g., what one person calls a Flemish-garden wall bond may be known as a Sussex bond by another). By studying suitable books on brick and stone laying, you will see a host of brick bonds for walls. Make sure to choose one that complements your house, but be aware a stretcher bond wall is only (so-called) a half-brick thickness, and is easily pushed over; unless so, its strong pillars are built-in along its length. Any mortar splash must carefully remove from the face of the stone. Here, there is a list of some popular bonds:

- Flemish Bond Flemish Garden Wall Bond
- English Bond English Garden Wall Bond
- Various Wall Brick Bonds Brickwork Joints

The style of joint between the bricks in the garden wall is important. A selection of brick joints is:

- The flush joint
- The weather-struck and cut joint
- The overstruck joint
- The rounded-tooled-concave joint
- The recessed joint
- The raked joint.

A brick 'header 'bond' wall

A flush joint is where the mortar is flush with the face of wall. And such a joint cause the wall bricks to blend in with the garden wall and not to stand out so much as individual items. The weathered-struck and the cut joint is where the pointing trowel blade is run along with the mortar between the bricks and sloped so that water runs away from the face of the wall. Then there is the rounded-tooled-concave joint, which is achieved by running a special tooling, or galvanized bucket handle, along with the wet mortar, so that an impressed trough is left on the wet mortar. The recessed joint is where, for example, a piece of wood is so cut to produce a tongue of wood that will run inside the joint space between the bricks, removing all the mortar to a depth of 12 mm. This makes each brick stand out. The raked joint is a shallower version of this. On some old cottage garden walls, a form of pointing known as tuck-pointing was used. The bricks' mortar was colored the same color as the bricks and brought to a flush finish. Then, thin 3 mm troughs of white mortarwere inserted into the joints' pliable brick mortar at a suitable time, the work being done by a consummate craftsman.

By studying the walls of your house, most probably, you notice that all the brickwork perpends (vertical joints) are never directly above another perpend (vertical joint); the perpend is often in the middle of the brick below it, which gives greater strength to the wall. There many brick colors, faces and forms; however, it is important to consider the house wall bricks you have already in your garden, as mix them with other ones may create an odd effect (but, of course, this not necessarily the case). Usually, you can find the bricks you like best at your local shops and, possibly, at your local garden centers or landscaping yard. It is imperative to clean up the face of wall so that no brick mortar is an allowed to dry on the wall's face: the mortar that has dried on the wall's face could ruin the overall effect your wish to create.

Buying Your Supplies

Now we move into the doing instead of the thinking, at least for a bit. That's because now we need to go shopping and start buying the supplies we'll need for our gardens. In addition to reading the materials in this book, I suggest you also listen to the seals people's opinion at the flea markets and various shops, and talk to your neighbors: you may find cheaper (or more beautiful) materials that now you don't remember. By pooling the other people's resources, you'll save not only time, but also supplies and money. How might you save on supplies? For example, if you and your neighbor split the cost, you can each buy different items and share them. By buying different types of seeds and mixing and matching, you can create something unique: 'just you'.

So, where exactly do you start? In the sale ads gardening section: take advantage of the periods in which there will be items on sale or reduced in this section (for example, because the shop is selling off, to make room for the next supply of anything). This means sales and markdowns, and maybe even bargaining to get the best items for a better price!

Other places where you'll often find lower-priced unique items are at places such as the 0.99 cent store, as well as even thrift stores, and flea markets. Once you have bought the supplies you need, you'll want to clean and sterilize them, if there is any residue on the containers. Let them dry overnight before you plant things in them and place them where you want. If you are a creative type and are into recycling your things this is the perfect time to get rid of those old shoes, bottles or anything else which is waterproof as long as you sterilize them and let them dry first; like when we were in school, we saved our milk containers, and used to put our beans or other plants inside to grow them.

One a rainy day you could even decorate a plain container with papier-mâché and colorful paper. This is great, especially if you have children who want to stay entertained on a day, they have to stay in. Anything is possible when you have a bit of creativity and time. If you still want a beautiful no muss, no fuss garden, there are several options you can choose from. These are especially great if you are concerned with the environment; after all, why are you recycling, am I right?

If you want the beauty of a green lawn without the fear of wasting water or fertilizer running off into the street and sewer, I may just have the answer you are looking for. I am a water waster watcher, and it drives me crazy to just hear or see water running for no reason whatsoever when washing dishes, or seeing it run off into the street and into the sewers; so, these ideas and suggestions are perfect for those who subscribe to the same way of thinking as I do.

One idea is to create herb gardens that line a walkway to your door. Herbs such as rosemary, thyme, sage, and mint, can cover bare ground and are useful for flavoring and fragrance. Another way is to create walkways and what is known as living carpets instead of grass. Living carpets do not need water, mowing or fertilizer. How awesome is that? For the east side of your house, you might consider planting sweet woodruff in a moist and shady place. Some other plants' ideas for yards include a yellow flowering bush called sedum, blue finger and velvet rose.

Co-founder of the team blog Garden Rant and founder of The Lawn Reform, Susan Harris, says that gardening is a dynamic form of art and counts on keeping it alive. She goes on to say, "the soul of the gardener", and I agree. As with art, painting a garden expresses what the person who created it felt and who they were!

Let's together see how we can create your awesome garden!

Chapter 4: Tips to work as a Landscaper professional

A garden can be a spectacular paradise or an unfinished hellhole. This is typically the first because you do not reside to hold the equipment to bedding plants breathing in the greenhouse. There are several options to update your garden quickly without calling in a landscaper for any ragged landscaping. We've put together quick tips and easy ideas for planting, which will make your room brighter. So that will make up half the time it takes to mow the grass in!

Create Your Own Hanging Basket

When you've got an old glass jar at home, making it to an eye-catching, drooping shelf is fun. All you need to do is add a covering, two strings, some fertilizer, a couple of flowers, and you're finished.

Look Outside the Current System

You can change the current look of your garden, even if all neighbors have a similar style to each other. You can get yourself an old shelf set or a budget-friendly seedlings cabinet to spruce up your indoor greenhouse.

Make sure your seat and benches are weather-resistant and last for summers and winters; why not try to make them lovely up with some bright paint?

Enhance the Garden Look with a Reflector

Buy spotlights with a weather-resistant mirror and place them to establish a focal light where you want more attention. Using spotlights can optically increase the impression of space in a small enclosed courtyard or create more a romantic atmosphere.

Buy Synthetic Grass

If you are looking for a lush green garden, but haven't the perseverance or the time to keep it trimmed and watered, then the remedy is fake turf. Usually, you don't even have to be afraid to your neighbors think your lawn is fake, thanks to some super-realistic prototypes. Just be sure to clean it, with a rough bristled rag every so often.

Grow your Companion Plants to Grow Specific Materials

Some preliminary tests are required for the user key. Usually, you can look at the mixes that the plants have in your neighborhood: they can grow only near the plants that make their survival possible, so you can see the ones that already exist. For starters, as the fragrance deters blackfly, well-smelling herbs like thyme grow alongside roses well.

Put Garden Technology to Use

When you can't really rely on ensuring that your plants are well-tended and well-cared, it may be time to look at a pot of self-watering plants. There are loads of devices planted out there to make your land plot simpler to navigate: you might as well use an electronic pot soon!

Overcrowding

Planting right is very important but knowing when to prune or not prune is fundamental. Enable your mint to expand out of its plant container; if the Alpine Heather is unruly, it'll be safer to keep it more unchanged. Give the daily pruning rest and create a garden area for your pruning experiments. The real keys things in gardening are: keeping plants well fed, giving the plants the right space and giving them a little love.

Succulent 'Indisposable Plants'

Do not keep the soil absolutely clean and dry, as this will deliberately kill the plants. Try investing in near-indestructible succulents that can be managed without a standard water system. However, if you want a fragrant flower, Jasmine is a surprisingly strong plant that can withstand unfavorable conditions; however, it needs some water in arid conditions.

Use this Hack on a Bin Liner

Forget toxic weed killers and time-consuming pruning: keep in mind this suggestion if your garden doesn't seem to be able to eliminate its weed problem. Fill the garden over the weed-ridden field with a bin cover frame, and weigh it down with blocks; keep the sheet long enough to remove the air from the weeds, which will destroy themselves. Even the most untrained homeowner creates remarkable landscape-it does not need hours of energy.

Clearing Up of Floors

When is the best time to do a quick scrubbing and spruce the deck or fix grass up, a power washer can do the job in so little electricity -and the change is so gratifying!

Make Your Deck a Place to Lounge In

If you are going to build a relaxing area, you can invest in an outdoor sofa; up the comfort level with luscious cushions, dining chairs, and an outside blanket, and get the most out of a gazebo, that shade you in the hottest seasons.

Cheer up Empty Bench

To do a second life to your landscape bench, try to move it into a new location and build a nice environment where you can chill and rest. You can dress it up with a lot of cushions and a chair cover and you could spruce it up with fresh paint colors. If you love the sidebar, you can create a stand near the bench as a bar table, to drink a cooler cocktail.

Establish a Drinking-Station

The iced coolers are simple-to-fill soda dispenser, and you can place on a wooden shelf while you're having fun outside; this suggestion could use to you to maintain the drinks cooled during the summer parties.

Brickwork Mix

Give an old garden wall a facelift by seeding shrubs through its gap. Add grit to the planting location pushing through the wall the plant species, and wait for them to be settled. Remember than very seldom grow the sedums and sempervivums.

Choose What Seat to Turn In

A baffling seat you have in the house can be enjoyed outdoor, creating a little paved space with two or three seats to sit in for just one or two people: it makes a more casual and intimate atmosphere, regardless of the environment, especially if you add a table with some candles on it, and you cover the seat with comfortable fabric and velvet cushions.

Flowers or Bulbs in Pots and Tin

Why waste a ton on planter boxes when you can create a beautiful series with reclaimed jam jars and food tins? Pay attention only to their eventual dangerous areas: remove or level them and you can use jars without problems. To drain your plant well, drill holes on the base jar and place it on top of some layers of stone blocks.

When Gardening Starts

Don't mind finding an appropriate plot in your yard: just start a garden wherever you like, as long as the soil is healthy and the weeds stop fast! If you want to start in a little section of your garden, you can create a raised garden. If your container garden were outside your back door or a frequently used doorway, it would be more likely to carry your planting through. First, start low, then work up into a larger yard.

Proper Treatment of the Manure and Solid Land

You can create a bin only for manure to fertilize soil and plants naturally. Ensure that the bin contains enough soil and is in a ventilation area, especially if lots of manure is implied. You can also put the food waste in it: composting your meal waste, as eggshells, coffee grindings, and apple cores, is easy.

Place of the Site

Some plants require shade, others need sunny weather, yet more plants require both shade and sunshine! Due to these facts, you don't have to overlook part of an overview of your farm! Even if you are a beginner gardener, you can have the best solution: if you are undecided if a plants need shade or sun, take and place it in a container garden on tires or a trolley: you can push it around if it doesn't receive as much (or too much) sunshine as you think.

Schedule and Styling

When you intend to grow with greenhouse plants, every sort of plant species needs to be planted at the right moment. When you have chosen to grow your plants in your area, make sure you plan them at the correct time of year and, to understand when plant right, make sure to test the seed details too; usually, the seasons in which a seed must be sown are spring or summer.

Well Irrigated

Make sure you send more than enough moisture to small seedlings and yet avoid wetting the plant leaves! Wet leaves may also quickly contribute to decay, mold, and make the plant sick! Remember that, in growing the sprouts, the major part of plants needs a little more than one inch of water a week. There's barely any effort to pop up and give your plants some water as you leave the garden outside of your house. Look for holly bushes in your local zone: they indicate frequent heavy rainfall!

Taking an Organic Push

The keys are: follow your landscape project, choose the rights plants, fertilize them and monitor pests, and enjoy your land with expected results. Remember: the use of natural fertilizer develops plants that are much more flavorful and healthier than normal forms; instead, plants that are fertilized or chemically treated can decay and become susceptible to disease.

Chapter 5: Types of gardening

Before talking about gardening types, we look at some main aspects you keep in mind in your landscape project creation. Your garden can help encourage and sustain a comfortable life and can also contribute to your wellness as well as others that may live in the surrounding. To maintain a healthy garden, the usage of organic materials is of the utmost importance. Organic materials also assist in buffering variations in temperature; for example, organic mulches. There are all different kinds and types of mulches. Some of the common examples are pine bark, wood chips, sawdust, etc. Organic mulches or any kind of vegetation covering the ground will prevent the soil/ground from rapidly heating up in the hot weather. In cold weather, it would prevent the ground from turning too cold. It also helps maintain the moisture in the soil, minimizes water loss, and provides the plants with necessary nutrients, which is a key in keeping your plants and overall your garden/landscape healthy. The trees help to protect against excessive heat and piercing sunlight and also aids in protecting against unfavorable weather conditions, for example, extremely cold winds or frost. Seasonal trees are also known as **deciduous trees** and shed their leaves during winters, inviting the sunlight to keep the surrounding warm and comfortable; regrow their leaves during summer to provide with shade, and make the overall temperature cooler comfort. Be mindful of which kinds of trees you choose and of which variety for your landscape! Refrain from choosing roots that are not very invasive: place your trees with a little bit of distance following your house-building or paving, so there are fewer chances of root damage; also, choose your spot carefully, where fallen branches and leaves do not pose a problem or discomfort. Another important aspect: colors have a psychological impact on people in general. They are set into two groups: *warm colors* that include orange, red, yellow, and *cool colors* that include mostly green, blue, pastel colors. Warm ones usually encourage a person psychologically to become active, whereas cool ones give an overall relaxing atmosphere. It is a good idea to place warm-colored flowers/plants where you usually work, and cool colored flowers/plants should be placed where you usually sit and relax. Scents emitted from many certain plants also have significant medical advantages; for example, herbs such as mints and thyme act as decongestants because they help in clearing nasal activities and prevent any blockage (minutely). At the same time, some plants may promote allergies such as Amaranth, ordinary sunflowers, Daises. Allergies can give hay fever and severe headaches, especially if the garden's ventilation is not well kept. About the garden machinery, the usage of these can cause disturbance to neighbors, who are trying to relax or sleep; it also invests in air pollution, which is not good for health. Instead of using machinery, hand tools are a better alternative, and you could always use some extra exercise for refreshment and fitness. For example, you can use ax and handsaw instead of a chainsaw, and hand-pushed mower than a powered land one. Regular cutting keeps the grass healthy and prevents you from the discomfort of cutting long grasses, which is tiring. Avoid using powered trimmers and use hedging shears in place of it to trim plants. Use a scythe in place of brush cutter. Keep any garden machinery you're using well maintained as it will reduce fumes and noise and so it does not pose as a disturbance to others. The usage of incinerators should be avoided, no matter what: it will not only contribute to air pollution, but when the air blows, it will disturb you as well as your neighbors because of the many toxins and fumes it contains that are very harmful to health and is not pleasant in the slightest.

Formal Garden Design

Formal gardens are architectural, symmetric, impressive and magnificent. This classic gardening design emerged in Persia. Islamic classical courtyard gardens, Asian Mughal gardens, Renaissance Art gardens, elaborate French Parterre, and Elizabethan era English knot orchards are all variants of this type. With a few preparation tips and a clear understanding of this style, you will build your own structured backyard privacy.

Advantages of a Formal Garden

- At first, formal gardens can appear to entail a lot of effort, but they also deliver some really good landscape advantages. This garden style is suitable for a limited plot because it provides an illusion of scope, bringing beauty to the home; since plantings are small in size, they can be effectively preserved in optimal historical circumstances.

- Except for annual flower beds, all trees and shrubs are central components, keeping recurring costs low.
- The formal garden is really calming for the body and mind.

Planning a Formal-Style Garden

Throughout the design and implementation processes, correct preparation is needed: you must consider the scale and form of the greenhouse, its functional intent, and the land's natural features.

1) Preparing the Land

What you need to plan the plot for a formal garden is a perfect flat natural landscape. Through earth-moving machinery, slight unevenness may be quickly eroded. When there are significant level variations, plan a two-story stepped garden.

2) Defining the Perimeter

You may use a square or rectangular plot to create a beautifully symmetrical landscape, but a frequently formed field must be trimmed.

Tall hedges or tall walls can divide up the garden area from the plot. The main gate can have to be moved to fall straight from the house's main entrance, becoming the garden's central component.

3) Planning the Layout

Ideally, the model will be drawn on paper with precise proportions because it will be brought to the initial execution site. For main geometric patterns, select a square, circle, or rectangle. Stretching strings over stakes in the field will help you draw straight lines from the land map.
Symmetry is an essential element of any formal garden: therefore, the areas on either end of the central axis should be designed as mirror images. When the garden is designed to attract visitors, plan to have wide-open spaces and seating areas_to talk with them. Wrought iron furniture combines with a formal landscape very well.

Major Features to Include in your formal garden

The elements that distinguish this landscape theme are:

Pathways

The central path absolutely has to pass around the main axis, determining the garden's bilateral symmetry. Other smaller paths can branch off. They may be graved or paved, usually filled with low hedges.

Focal point

Installed either in the center of the garden or at an end, a water body, an unusual figure, a new sculpture or a big tree may act as a focal point.

Water feature

Although water is not so necessary, it is welcome. Consider installing a swimming pond, a stream flowing down the main road, or even a big birdbath.

Vertical appeal

Establish vertical value by incorporating topiaries, standard-trained or straight-line trees, and stone or stone pillars with decorative or wide urns. Be very sure to use such features to prevent cluttering.

Greenery

Greenery is the foundation of a formal landscape, usually as trimmed hedges, shrubbery, and lawns. This well-manicured appearance is vital: leave the grass mowed and neatly clipped. Quick-to-shape bushes and plants with naturally smooth forms are favored. Use low-maintenance xerophytes (plants which can tolerate droughts) is a recent phenomenon of formal gardens.

Moderate Colors

Formal gardens use a minimal paint range. Annual and annual beds may be positioned in rectangular patterns in the center of lawns, or installed around the hedges as one-foot-wide beds. They must be planted together for a pleasant feel using only two to three harmonious colors. You might want to add a few trees as seasonal color highlights.

Plant Suggestions

The following are the plants that work perfectly in a formal garden.

Topiary and Hedges: Yew, Rosemary, Boxwood, Arborvitae, and Privet

Bushes: Thuja, Ficus, Junipers, Brunfelsia, and pencil Cypress

Trees: Crabapple, Cherry, Dogwood, and fan Palms

(Arborvitae – Thuja – Ficus)

Annuals: Tulips, Salvias, Marigolds, Calendulas, Asters, and Begonias.

Perennials: Hydrangea, Lavender, Nepeta, Echinacea, and Daffodils.

Low-maintenance plants: Yucca, Cycads, Agave and date Palms

(Marigold – Lavender)

Informal Garden Design

Informal gardens are the most growing garden type; with their natural alignment, the intimate garden is also less restrictive. Informal gardening will liberate you from constraints such as awareness of comprehensive horticulture or architecture, and enabling you to 'visit' the gardening before you start. I always support novice gardeners to create the informal garden first, to start understanding every sort of gardening.

You will see what designs and patterns you want, create planting schemes, notice what works for you and what doesn't. An informal garden must be comfortable and open. Others say casual garden architecture gives more border flexibility and encourages planting to have the foundation instead of hard landscaping.

However, an informal landscape design should not be confused with gardens that are disjoined, with colors and borders that slapdash together, or features that occur randomly in gardens. These are things that are prevented by landscape planners. The iterating and placed of plants should seem “casual”; however, it must have his logic. During their preparation, open garden architecture requires as much effort and patience as a formal garden: planning, harmony, equilibrium, size, proportion, correct features and plants in the right position. Everything seems effortless but must be done cautiously. Looking at the UK's adjacent landscapes, you can quickly identify informal landscape projects. Informal implies that the garden implements even looser patterns and curves and typically takes its architecture from land layers.

You should trace the site boundary lines, road, house walls, lake, and trees collection and where the sun spreads its warm rays. You can see mixed borders of beautiful plant drifts and exotic plants mixed with the local ones. The informal garden style is far from that of a formal garden's order and its razor accuracy. Informal gardens are not inclined to follow formal gardens rules, allowing a whole different and unexpected style to blow up. The sky might be the only limit.

How to create an informal garden?

- Mixing different palettes and colors
- Use other products than rough rectangular landscaping
- Adopt curves and smoother lines
- Allow further planting and diversity
- Create a comfortable and free lines
- Use asymmetry in your project
- Mixing cohesive materials

Who, do informal gardens are supposed to appeal to?

Informal gardens will cater to fewer citizens who are more in line and appreciate nature on finding its path. Styles for informal gardens like cottage garden and meadow planting encourage plants to mix and develop together. Although forms should be used, they are not inherently symmetrical or centered on any axis; for example, informal gardens may often be divided in half and might also be combined. In simple words, casual gardens are very comfortable and less deliberate.

But this doesn't make them any easier to manage or maintain!

Here are some typical conclusions that are recommended for an informal style garden.

- Mix the plants together.
- Keep the natural topography and lines of the garden
- Use natural products for planting and surrounding
- Allowing the garden to grow over a while.
- For those who want 'laid back type': if it's not finished today, there's still tomorrow!

Water features for informal gardens

In informal gardens informal, wildlife, natural ponds, water features are allowed. Use natural materials and gentle curves; natural water will become the garden's emphasis, and it could attract animals and neighbors' eyes. However, remember that a poorly built or improperly shaped informal pond will look terrible, making your garden look messy.

Informal landscape management

Maintenance, like every landscape, relies on plants and nature. When you're going to create a home garden filled with summer flowers, ensure that care should be intense, and seed flowers are primed for the season. Though, informal gardens that have slow-growing shrubs and evergreens areas may be comparatively free of maintenance. It is a good idea to design casual gardens as a year-round color combination with limited pruning. The problem of a poorly designed informal garden is that of the 'pick and choose' planting commonly done as people slowly add plants and flowers in their backyard, which bloom at various times, which might end up in a continuous maintenance process. It's also important to carefully consider the height and increasing pace; for example, a lovely little perennial, growing, could take over the tiny boundary! A carefully planned garden plan prevents this and provides the landscape a year-round framework that fits your degree of involvement!

The Pitfall of Informal Gardens

Create something without order, purpose, and preparation, I think that can often be the undoing of not only an informal garden, but of any garden; an informal garden without logic or purpose may only quickly become a "messy garden". Don't fill your garden with every type of items, just because these have been sold in low-price! Don't fill your garden with too many plants (one too close to each other), as they may grow against each other and dry out; for example, if you plant Azalea and cactus too close, or a tropical plant in a too cold area, one of them could not survive.

Chapter 6: Landscaping with Annuals

Important tools for your perfect garden design

To make a great gardening project, you have to know which tools you need. Moreover, you must understand some important characteristics of your garden. You should have handly:

- Shovel
- Spade
- Spading fork
- Scythe
- Trowel
- Scraper
- Rake
- Shears
- Pruners
- Hose
- Water equipment
- Hedge trimmers
- Lawn sprinklers
- Vases

First of all, to create a strong and durable garden, you should understand what type of soil there is in your yard, and what type of plants you should plant, according to the local whether, dry air, winds and frequents of rain. There are three mains types of soil:

- **Clay soil**: its minuscule and thick particles garner a lot of dampness; when water in earth soil depletes, it gradually becomes compact.
- **Sandy soil** is opposite to clay one; water (and also its significant supplements) effectively travels through its particles; then is a less nutritional and more arid soil.
- **Topsoil** is perfect for most plants; its particles garner the right amount of water and nutrients; moreover, it is wealthy in humus, an element that decays quickly.

Questions for you to understand the best plants for your garden

- Which types of plants are growing in my region naturally?
- What whether conditions are the most prevalent here? Cold, or warm seasons? Humid or dry air? Strong winds or breeze? Does it rainy often? Are the rains strong and sudden, or are they calm but frequent?
- What native plant hybrids are available for seeding there?
- What type of plants are indigenous there?

Gardening is a progressing procedure; while timing is critical, don't be overpowered by a feeling of being past the point where it is possible to plant by some discretionary date.

Summer

Gardening is a progressing procedure. While timing is critical, don't be overpowered by a feeling of being past the point where it is possible to plant by some discretionary date. Summer season demands a lot of care and protection from insects, pests and the heatwaves; therefore, plants must be handled with care during this period of the year.

Some of the plants that can be planted during this season are as follows:

- Beetroot
- Broccoli
- Pansies
- Snapdragons
- Dianthus
- Petunias
- Bush beans
- Fuchsias
- Mangoes
- Apricot
- Bitter gourd
- Ladyfinger
- Bringle

As we said earlier, summer season requests a great deal of consideration and insurance from bugs and the warmth waves; plants must be maneuvered carefully amid this time of the year. Before starting summer, you should ensure that you keep seedlings watered in dry pots. Continue sowing in late summer and harvest time; a large portion of these veggies will develop outside cheerfully even as the climate turns colder. Any support you can offer will help for later sowings as harvest time goes ahead: scaled-down plastic and wool passages are a simple present-day other option to customary cloches. Frequently simply keeping chilly winds off your plants, by raising protection panels near the little plants, is all that is expected to give you a truly fruitful harvest. If, however, you are sufficiently fortunate to have a nursery or polytunnel, don't let it get exhausted once your midyear products are out; feed it and keep using it. Consider putting on the infant plants and seedbeds outdoors to transplant them covert by the tomatoes, peppers and cucumbers, which you have already trimmed. In a passage/nursery you can sow servings of mixed greens and greens consistently.

Tips and techniques

- Plants in this season are sensitive to pesticide attacks, because they are dried easier. Therefore, the plants must be checked regularly and thoroughly and water them frequently so that the plant is not too water drained.
- Use a complete package of lawn fertilizers: these fertilizers must fulfill the demands of nitrogen, phosphorus, sulfur, and potassium.
- Observe the plants and check if there is any attack of pests on your plants.
- Apply the right amount (but not too much) moss repellents; use pest control, instead of chemical repellents, to avoid damage to the plantation.
- Keep yourself alert if snails hurt the plants, damaging them.

Although summer is the most crucial time period of every year, during which many living things get damaged due to high-intensity scorching heat generated by sun rays over the earth's surface, it is a great time for your lawn in many senses. During this time the flowers and plants will be in full bloom and the grass will be lush green, but plenty of weeds would also be there to create some chaos. You have to pay attention to the weeds formation during summers to protect the plants and flowers and beautify the lawns in general. Make the following tasks will help you to protect your lawn in summer:

- Weeding the lawn at least twice a week
- Trimming leaves on plants and shrubs
- Mowing the lawn timely

- Remove the thatch whenever necessary
- Adding lawn decorations and other landscaping
- Watering the lawn and cleaning out the corners and porch railings

Planting to create some shady areas over other shade-need plants is also very useful to protect them from direct sun burn during the hottest season of the year. Planting drought-resistant plants in open areas, weeding the lawn timely, mowing the lawn and covering it with straw (that dampens the heat) are some tasks that will help retain the wellness of the plants and flowers growing inside the garden. You can do this by yourself, or you might have to ask a professional like lawn care, which could help you do the hardest homework.

Autumn

Fall is a decent time to get into the garden. In this period, your soil contains a reasonable amount of warmth from summer before the winter downpours hit, so it's an extraordinary time to get planting. Interestingly, one can get extremely creative with the garden at this point of the year. To prepare the gardening calendar for this season, you must make sure to sow all those seeds that demand nothing else but full sun, room to grow and bright sunlight.

Some of the plants that are usually grown during this season are as follows:

- Brassicas
- Peas
- Lettuce
- Leeks
- Onions
- Asian pears
- Date plum guava
- Grapes
- Pineapple
- Swiss chard
- Turnips

However, to make a complete blooming garden some techniques must be kept in mind while gardening, as these explained follow.

Tips and techniques

Following tips and techniques must be kept in mind while preparing an autumn garden.

Plant fruit trees

The weather during the autumn season is ideal for planting fruits and vegetables. However, you should avoid overcrowding all of the other plants as well as structures including fences: this will curb the growth of these plants.

Addition of Mulch

Mulch is the best friend of your garden; this will keep the soil moist, therefore, avoiding the need for watering plants by you. Moreover, it will keep the weed concentration low. You can use the classical mulch, but there is some inexpensive substitute you can use in your garden; you will explore them later.

Use fertilizer

Preparing your lawn will guarantee that it stays green and solid consistently. Harvest time is an incredible time to treat since it secures your grass through the winter months; due to this fact, you should prepare your land very well twice every year (in autumn and spring) for the best results.

Prune trees

There are numerous reasons why you ought to prune your trees. it enhances your trees' well-being and appearance, expels dead or dried branches and can also advance tree uptake of natural product.

Plant evergreens

Evergreens frame the foundation of a greenhouse, giving the structure a permanent interest; thus, the more evergreens in your patio nursery, the better it will look in winter! With warm soil and cooler conditions, harvest time is the perfect time to fill those holes in your edges. Sarcococca and Daphne will bring green leaves with beautiful reflections, and delightfully fragrant blooms in the profundities of winter. For a rich bigger bush take a stab at spring blossoming Camellias or Fatsia for its expansive engineering foliage; for a more formal look, why not put resources into some crate or yew topiary: Lonicera Nitida, Bay and Holly can likewise be cut into formal shapes and make astounding evergreen fences as well.

Winter

Preparing the garden to bed for the winter is, for the most part, a matter of tidying up and concealing. As fall advances and temperatures drop, those plants that aren't murdered by and large by ice get ready for lethargy. Get out the darkened stems and foliage of yearly blossoms and vegetables to keep the likelihood of their harboring malady pathogens and bug eggs over the winter. The cool climate in which some plants become an icy casing, and you can dive plants into mulch, and box other ones in raised beds. You can also make general repairs in the garden. Doubtlessly, the natural mulch you spread to secure the dirt amid the mid-year months has disintegrated. It's imperative to spread new mulch at the beginning of winter, in a thicker layer, to secure plants and soil over the winter months. The key is to keep the soil "dirty" and warm to keep the temperature even, and mulch is perfect due to its thermal-insulating capacity. Indeed, once the dirt is solidified, mulch keeps it solidified, and it maintains the temperature. So, if you have shade trees, use the fallen leaves to mulch and utilize it all through your property.

These are some plants that grow during the winter:

- Broad beans
- Kohlrabi
- Lettuce
- Onions
- Rhubarb
- Strawberries
- Berries
- Currants

Tips and techniques

The short days and severe climate can make the possibility of planting in winter both ugly and conceivably useless. However, a smidgen of winter arranging can get the garden prepared for an awesome year ahead.

Clean

Accumulate all the instruments you have utilized in the course of recent months and properly cleaning to evacuate all the earth and rust. Utilize a gentle cleanser to sterilize pots and seed plates.

Check walls and alike

Look at the walls, sheds, entryways, and different structures for shortcoming or spoil indications and get them repaired before the snow and high winds arrive.

Garden Care

The garden needs somewhat of a breather over the winter months, so keeping the grass out is the best thing to do; make an exception to dispose of the huge weeds, greenery and clears out.

Storehouses

Give sheds and nurseries a decent scour and sort out each of those greenery enclosure instruments you cleaned before. Spruce up tables and seats also.

Lists

To spend a chilly winter's night, the best approach can be poring over a good portion of the numerous seeds you can plant in winter, on the inventories, longing for the developing season to come, and arranging your optimal greenery enclosure.

Cover the plants, but also the gardener!

We have already talked earlier about the importance of cover the soil; protect the seeds in the soil with mulch, is one of the best ways to maintain life sprouts until spring. During the winter, plants may fall due to strong wind, and it is important to ensure that fauna can find shelter into trees or vegetations near your garden; however, keep in mind the importance of the gardener's healthy! Dressing fittingly and ensuring yourself against the rigors of winter ought to be one of your first contemplations; then, remember to buy a heavy dress, thick gloves and a raincoat. If there are inclined trees in your garden, keep I mind blocking them by a strong branch against, to prevent them from falling above you! Moreover, whatever you do with the bulbs at the start of autumn, their survival depends on three factors: bulb tenacity, bulb planting depth, and the possibility or not of frost in your area. For colder environments, you'll need to keep your seeds aloft (in a less cool and sunny place, not in contact with the ice on the ground, until the danger of ice has passed – for example, a nursery). In case you have to leave them in the ground during the winter, start in the autumn to replant deeper all your sprouts and give them the right control during the winter.

Spring

Plants that typically blooms in Spring season are

- /Cherry Plant
- Almond tree
- Magnolia
- Wisteria
- Roses
- Primrose
- Hawthorn (Crataegus /Monogyna)

Tips and Techniques

Cold Frames, Cloches and Polytunnels

If you live in the colder northern climates particularly, often even in the Spring season there is too cold yes, then getting cloches, trenches, or polytunnels organized is essential if you want to start. If you already have a **trench**, you should straighten up the old frame, cover over with soil again and tamp down. The cover is then sunk into the opposite side and pulled down tight on the frame, and then you fill the trench. The ends are pulled around and fixed to the wooden door-frame, or pulled down and into a trench around a **polytunnel** end. These simple and relatively cheap constructions offer a possibility for growing a good selection of early and late vegetables. If there is too cold or you want to quicken the plants' growth, the addition of a **Hot Bed** along one side can give you a fantastic early start to your vegetable growing. Plants within the polytunnel will also benefit from this early start to the season.

Spring is also a time to get the **cold frames** cleared out and prepared to accept your young plants or seeds. However, remember not to be too enthusiastic when it comes to sowing seeds early on in the Spring! A late frost can soon reduce your efforts to nothing – especially if you have forgotten to cover them over at night with garden fleece or even loose dry straw to protect them. Several garden centers make a fortune by selling early plants to over-keen gardeners, who don't realize that plants they have bought have lived forced-on for a long time in heated polytunnels. They soon perish when planted out with these ideal conditions, because plants don't support temperature range– meaning that the plants have to be repurchased!

Cold Frames and cloches do not have to be great works of construction; simply make a frame raised on one side to catch the early sun and cover over with an old window or polypropylene sheet to cover the plants. Originally, people used a bell-shaped glass structure (much loved by the Victorians); currently, we use a modern-day cloche, that is a simple structure to cover rows of seedlings – like a mini-polytunnel. This can be made from wire hoops or plumbers plastic pipe stuck into the ground to form a tunnel.

Raised beds should be moved on according to the shady and sunny areas to freshen them up, and new composting material should be addedevery

week. Do not use topsoil in a Raised Bed garden if at all possible, as this tends to firm-up and defeat the main objective of a Raised Bed Garden – which should be easy to dig and maintain. Traditional vegetable garden beds should be plowed with a shovel or a fork before the last of the winter frost; frost, indeed, helps to break up the soil and also to kill

destructive pests that have over-wintered in the soil. If you are fortunate enough to have a pig or two, then let them root around in the ground for a week or so before planting. They will happily root out any grubs and slugs hiding in the soil – and fertilize the ground in the process! Chickens are also quite good for this, as they will scratch around all day looking for insects and grubs.

Crop Rotation

In order for any vegetable patch to prosper and give out the best results, general rules must be observed, and perhaps the most important of these are crop rotational rules. Crop rotation is a gardening practice that consist of growing different types of plants in the same area during the season sequence; it is essential to maintain the right nutrient amount and control pest and weed pressure. You must bear in mind that each plant belongs to one specific *family*; similar family components feed by similar soil nutrients. For instance, tomato and potato are in the same *family* and so will attract the same pests and use up the same soil nutrients: this, of course, means that they should be planted separately wherever possible. Another example is to plants carrots and onions in the same place in which there was planted garlic before. The goal of proper crop management is that don't deplete the soil nutrients by planting vegetables with the same requirements, either together or following one after the other; for this reason, it is important also to know the *families* to which they belong.

Seed Propagation

Planting from seed may perhaps be a daunting thought for some, as it can be quite laborious and fraught with potential failure! However, by following the tips in this section, you will find that one of the great advantages is that you can 'steal a march' on the seasons and get a good early start to your veggie garden. Other reasons for choosing to grow from seed is that it is much cheaper than purchasing young plants from the garden center. Planting from seed also means that you will have a larger choice of plants to choose from, as typically garden centers can only stock a limited choice of the more popular adult varieties.

Plant Protection

There are many things to consider especially early on in the season, when damaging frost and hungry critters compete for your young plants, then this section will offer tips and advice to protect your plants from both. Even in the early Spring, destructive pests such as cutworm can cause severe damage to early planted crops such as beans and peas; fortunately, the solutions to these problems are often quite simple. To protect your beans and peas from the ravages of cutworm or even nibbling mice, try growing them inside a cardboard toilet-roll insert. Alternatively, you can also use 1/34 plastic plumbers pipe cut to 4-inch lengths. These can be used year on year compared to the cardboard inserts which will only last a season – but are equally effective. Below you will see a picture of some plastic pipes you could install over your young plants if the mice were too determined to nibble them away!

The pipes do half of the work, though; bugs could gain access to the young plants if they really wanted to, climbing or flying – the pipes just make the proposition less attractive! Moreover, as the warmer weather of early spring progresses, then flying pests such as the cabbage moth or butterfly can become a real pest: before you know it, your brassicas are crawling with caterpillars, that will demolish your hard work in no time! The simplest way to deal with these and other pests is to cover your brassicas with either garden fleece or fine nylon netting: this is simple and 100% effective – providing you do the job properly and allow no areas for the butterflies to gain access-, and raised beds are particularly easy to cover in this way. However, doing everything (from covering your plants to creating pipes) will protect them more effectively. A row cloche is usually made by simple fencing-wire loops sunk into the ground at each end then covered over with insect mesh or polythene.

Floating row covers are similar to the row cloche, but instead of being fixed to wires, they are simply placed loosely over the plants, leaving enough room for the plant to grow. This cover is held down at the sides by sinking the material into the ground and covering with soil. If your plants are growing in an very exposed position, put up wind barriers to stop your plants 'burning', as the wind dehydrates them faster than they can replace the moisture; a wicker fence can look particularly attractive in a garden area, but any fence or barrier made from hazel or willow, for instance, will do the job.

Plant Support

As you may imagine, there are numerous ways to support your vegetables; but why do they need support?

There are several good reasons why some plants need support; here are 3 of them:

- **To prevent fruit-laden branches** from trailing on the ground, making the fruits vulnerable to insect or animal attack.
- **If fruits such as tomatoes** are not supported then the main – or fruit-bearing - stem will collapse, resulting in damage to the plant and loss of the fruits.
- **Supported plants** can also get the best benefit from the sunshine and air-flow (helps prevent mold) and pollinating insects.

With that said, Spring is the perfect time to either make repairs to your existing plant supports or indeed to make up new ones for the coming season. Some examples of supports for fruit and vegetable plants can be seen in the pictures below.

But there are numerous ways to support your plants and indeed many different materials that can be used to good effect. Fences, canes, poles and posts can all be used in conjunction with fencing wire, nylon netting or garden twine to effect some version of these examples.

Peas and beans must be supported using canes and/or nylon netting. Vegetables grown in straw bales can be easily supported and protected using the wires strung between to support one with a pole at each end. Beans, peas, cucumber, tomatoes are strong climbers and will happily grow up canes set at 5-6 feet high.

One of these arrangements can also be used for supporting raspberries and other climbing fruit bearers; their horizontal lines can be from 2 to 3 strings each side, typically. In most cases the wires or supporting strings are set at around 9-inches apart. The supporting posts must be anchored well enough to take the wires' strain as they are tensioned, and the plant's weight as the fruit begins to develop.

In older established, the frame-work and eventually old supporting canes should be thoroughly inspected and treated before the season begins to remove any over-wintering pests that may have taken up residence.

Chapter 7: Landscaping for Perennials

Perennials Gardening Ideas for Beginners

Perennials have a lifespan of many years, and therefore, effective planning is required in the beginning before planting them. The right planning will offer happiness to the gardener for many years, as well as a poor initial planning and management will be noticed for many years. Therefore, a beginner needs to have enough ideas and diverse information before getting into perennials gardening. Below are the things you should consider when starting a perennial flower garden.

Siting A Perennial Flower Garden

The location chosen for a perennial flower garden should be strategic. Remember that the garden will be in that location for many years and so it should not be interrupted in just a few years. When siting your strategic location, you should consider the type of flower planted in the garden. Similarly, the garden has aesthetic value, and then you should be careful not to particular structures or beautiful views; you have to measure until your plants grow height approximately.

Designing A Perennial Flower Garden

The design affects the overall look of the perennial flower garden. There are no pre-defined techniques for designing a flower garden; the design chosen primarily depends on what you want. Nevertheless, when implementing any given design, the gardener has to consider the type of perennial flower; it will bloom giving a specific color, and this has to link with other colors of the project. Other physical characteristics such as the height, width and the texture of the perennial plant affect the type of design chosen and the garden design for tall perennials is different from the groundcover perennials one.

Here are three tips you can follow to get a good flower garden design.

1) Make a Scale Drawing

Like in any other design, you will need to sketch what you have in mind. You can also opt to use garden-planning software to draw your garden. Use a convenient scale to capture all the significant details, and make sure to include your perennial flowers with their respective mature sizes (their width and height). After making your scaled drawing, review it to see if it's exactly what you intended it to be; if not, correct your mistakes to get what you want.

2) Match the Drawing with the Structures

Depending on your home's size and the structures surrounding it, choose the appropriate type of flower garden. If you have a bungalow, a cottage, or a ranch house, an informal mix of perennial flowers and wavy-edged beds will be more effective; for a large home with robust architectural designs, a formal perennial flowers arrangement and mix will be more convenient.

3) Try Implementing Your Design

Get a long string and use it to layout your proposed garden. Is it what you wished for? Try to find some objects with heights approximately equal to the perennial flowers that you will plant and lay them within your string's confines, in the exact places you plan to plant the flowers; this will help you visualize the garden and make corrections if there are any.

After following the above steps, you should have a good perennial flower garden design.

Selecting Perennials

When selecting perennial flowers, the primary goal is to get the plants that can give you continuous color throughout the seasons of the year. You need to have different varieties of the perennial flowers. Evergreen perennials are better to maintain the green color when winter comes. The plants you select should have different blooming periods i.e. some for spring, summer and some for fall.

Below are the things you should consider when selecting the perennial flowers for your garden.

1) Consider the color

The color you choose entirely depends on your taste. If you intend to communicate a certain information using your flower garden, you can opt to follow the color psychology. According to this, every color has its meaning: for instance, red color means passionate, bold and active; blue means honest, trustworthy, and secure.

2) Consider the plant dimensions

Every plant has its peak mature size. When selecting your perennial flower, think about its mature dimensions. Specifically, the height matters a lot; when planting your perennial flowers, place the tall plants at the back and the smaller ones in front, and the tallest plants could be used to create your garden border. As you have already seen when designing, even the other dimensions matter a lot; leave a reasonable space to grow them when making your design.

3) Mix different varieties of perennials

There are thousands of varieties of perennial plants, and you don't have to confine yourself to particular types of perennials. Varieties are more appealing to the eyes than just a single type; so, mix your flowers but ensure that they have similar physical characteristics.

4) Match the perennials with their blooming periods

Since what you want is continuous blooming throughout all the seasons, then you have to get plants that can bloom throughout the seasons or some plants for each season. There are the extended-blooming perennials, early-blooming perennials, mid-season and late-blooming perennials,and you should have some plants from every category to have a continuous blooming. In the following paragraph, I'll give you some example of perennial plants and trees.

5) Match the perennials with the prevailing climatic conditions

Each perennial plant requires specific climatic conditions for its growth. How do you know if a plant can grow in your region? In all garden center, most plants are clearly labeled, and you have to buy the plant that can survive in your area. If your garden has a lot of shade, select those plants that can survive with less sunlight; likewise, if your garden is open, select plants that can survive a lot of sunlight. You should also consider the type of soil in your garden: if the soil is sandy you should be applying fertilizer regularly, but if the soil is moderately fertile, regular fertilizer application is unnecessary.

Types of Perennials

- Lavender
- Heuchera
- Dianthus
- Thyme
- Thrift
- Bee Balm
- Veronica (Speedweel)
- Ballon Flower
- Sedum
- Baptisia
- Peonies
- Catmint
- Dyalily
- Asters
- Salvia

Plants need shade: Astilbe, Geranium, Elleboro, Ajuga, Fern

Plants need sunlight: Coreopsis, Sedum, Echinops, Lantana Camara

Spring Blooming: Myositis Malva, Rosmarinus Officinalis, Juniperus

Winter blooming: Primuls, Lewisie, Forsizia (Sunlight), Aquifolium,

(Elleboro – Aquifolium)

Summer blooming: Echinacea, Achillea, Pervinca, Lavanda, Rosmarinus Officinalis, Juniperus

(Rosmarinus Officinalis – Echinacea)

Autumn blooming: Agnus-Castus, Ceratostigma Plumbaginoides, Plumbago capensis, Caryopteris

Prennials trees: Magnolia Grandiflora, Pinus, Abies, Cedrus Eucaliptus (needs sunlight)

(Abies – Agnus Castus – Magnolia)

Ground cover perennials: This type of plants could be one awesome element in your garden. They are essential in the border of flowerbeds, as they avoid the expansion of the weeds. These plants are very useful if in your garden are more levels and to decorate rocks; you can seed specific ground covers to recreate one specific world area landscape, as a dry climate zone. Ortensia – Lobelia – Thyme – Creeping Phlox - Alyssum – Lily – Lamium Maculatum

Propagating Perennials

If you followed the paragraph above, you should have a good idea about which perennial flowers you should plant for your garden. The only thing that remains is determining the method of propagation.

Perennials can be propagated by several means; the most common methods are the use of cuttings and rootstocks.

Use of cuttings

For this method, cut a soft stem about 6-inches long in early summer (leave about two leaves in the stem); dip the stem cuttings in a rooting hormone, and then place the cutting in a shallow container with soil mixed with peat. Wait for the cuttings to grow roots before transplanting them into your garden.

Use of rootstocks

This method involves dividing big perennials. For this method, wait for Spring when the perennials break into dormancy; uproot the wide plants, section them off into more pieces, and transplant each of them in the different sections. You can also opt to buy ready-made propagules, as long as they follow your selection criterion.

Maintaining a Perennial Garden

Once they are established, perennials require very minimal care. Despite this, there are several essential practices that the gardener should consistently do to keep his flower garden healthy and appealing. The essential routine maintenance practices include:

Irrigation

Perennials require frequent watering only when they are not fully established: during that time, they should be watered almost daily depending on the weather to help them develop and establish. When well established, perennials have extensive rooting, and they can access water deep in the soil; then, they may require slight watering at times to supplement the water they get from the soil. You can be watering by hand or using an irrigation system. The artificial solutions are perfect if you work many hours a day or leave for holidays because they allow you to set the time when water the garden. The manual one, though, allows you to sprinkle jets of water at angles and places where are difficult for the system to reach (for example, raised bed, flower bed, vertical garden).

During the **summer**, weekly watering will be needed, especially if the summer is so much dry. For sandy soil, little water should be used, but it should be more frequent. You can opt for one artificial irrigation method: drip and soaker hoses irrigation systems are the most efficient ones. Watering should be stopped at the onset of the **cooler seasons**.

Mulching

Immediately after planting the perennial flowers, mulching should be done to preserve the water applied; mulching should also be done even after the perennials are fully developed. Mulch should be applied at the onset of summer: this will prevent excessive evaporation of the irrigation water, keep the soil around the plant cool, and also act as a weeds control method. The mulch applied, though, should not alter the aesthetic value of your flower garden: fine materials such as dry grass, torn leaves, shredded bark, peanut shell, and cocoa hulls are more effective and less visible. Prevent the scattering of the mulch to retain the appealing nature of your flower garden.

Fertilizer Application

Well-established perennials need very little fertilizer to survive: most will react negatively to excess fertilization; moreover, excess fertilizer stimulates the production of excess foliage, thereby causes less blooming. The amount of fertilizer applied depends on the type of soil, and a soil test is usually necessary to identify the deficient nutrients. The results of the soil test will guide you on the type of fertilizer to apply. Slow-release fertilizers are more effective for perennials. Some methods of fertilizer application include broadcasting, topdressing, placement, foliar and aerial application; you can only choose the most convenient according to your lifestyle and also the soil. Usually, 1-3 pounds of nitrogen fertilizer per 1000 sq. ft. are enough for many perennials; still, for security, you have to listen to the center garden seller where you have bought the seeds or plants.

Manicuring

Shaping the flower garden should be a routine practice to maintain the aesthetic value, especially during summer. Some perennials such as Phlox, Aster, Salvias, and Chrysanthemums may sometimes be thin and leggy; such perennials require pinching off growing tips to limit upward growth and stimulate literal growth.

Some perennials develop many stems that may alter the design and also lower blooming; such perennials require regular pruning to maintain the design and encourage more blooms (production of many stems can also be avoided by removing the excess literal buds before they develop).

Some perennials such as hybrid Lilies and Delphiniums have a flexible stem that falls as they continue growing; those plants require staking to ensure that they take the gardener's design, to prevent the plant from diseases, and for better blooming. Such perennials can also be supported by inter-planting them with strong plants.

Other perennials such as Phlox, Daisies and Lavender do not drop the flowers after they dry up; these perennials may hold on to the dry flower for several seasons, reducing their blooming. Remove their deadheading will prolong their flowering period and also improve their aesthetic value.

Weed Control

Weeds provide unnecessary competition for nutrients and lower your flower garden's aesthetic value; regular weed control is, therefore, required. Bromegrass and quack grass are the most common weeds in perennial gardens. Several methods can be used to control weeds in a perennial garden. Weeds can be eliminated by regular flower garden's tilling, which also helps in the soil's loosening, encourages infiltration, and enhances aeration of the soil. Weeds can also be controlled by mulching because, besides keeping the soil cool and moist, it prevents the growth of weeds by blocking the sunlight. For mulching to be effective, it should be 2-inches deep. Herbicides such as glyphosate products may also be used to control weeds. Keep the right precautions when you use herbicides.

Pest Control

Each type of perennial flower has certain types of pests that affect it. Some pests have severe effects than the others, but they all have to be controlled. The methods of controlling pests vary depending on the type of pest affecting the perennial flowers; the most common pests that affect the perennial flowers include:

Aphids

These green or black insects cluster under the leaves and the stems of the perennial flowers and suck the plant's juice. Their symptoms include curled leaves, honeydew on the surface they have infected leaved, and distorted growth. The use of commercial insecticide can control Aphids, but a strong water stream may also be used to knock them from the plant, naturally.

Caterpillars

These are the intermediate larvae of several moths and butterfly species. They are of different sizes and colors, but they are easy to identify because they are leggy worms. Their infestation can be easily identified by the chewed leaves and sometimes totally missing leaves. There are commercial insecticides specifically for caterpillars, but I suggest you if the infestation is not severe, the caterpillars can be controlled by picking and moving them away.

Spider Mites

This type of pest use shielding webs underneath the leaves and then feeds and sucks on the leaves' juice. Their symptoms are color mottling, which appears as yellowing of leaves when seen from a distance, and the presence of webs underneath the leaves. Spider mites may be controlled by sprinkler irrigation because they prefer dry conditions.

Leaf miners

These are larvae stage insects that burrow underneath the leaf and feed on it; they can be easily identified with the zig-zag light lines on the leaf's upper surface resulting from their feeding. You can easily remove and move them away, if the infestation is not serious.

The other common pests that affect perennial flowers include slugs and snails, mealybugs, and whiteflies. To avoid heavy infestation of any of these pests, you should control and maintain the right amount of these; **not too many, but also not too few!** Snails, bugs and pests are not often damage, but on the contrary, in most cases they contribute to moving the soil, giving air to it; moreover, they are the prey of bigger animal, like birds, bats and lizards, that feed on them: so, I suggest you leave them to grow in your garden, to create the right ecosystem between plants, animals and pests. Use herbicides and pesticides only there is a big infestation in your garden, that you can't solve with other methods.

Disease Control

Perennials are also affected by several diseases, each of them is bad if not controlled, but some are severe than the others. Therefore, you should keep the flower garden in check all the time to identify a disease before it progresses.

The most common diseases that affect perennials include:

Damping Off

This is a fungal disease that infects the seedlings at the soil level: it restrains the stem and causes seedling's drying. Its symptoms include softening of the stem, falling off the plant, and death of the plant. This disease affects the perennial flowers before they develop fully; it can be controlled by ensuring that the flower garden is well-drained. For severe cases, a fungicide is more effective.

Leaf Spot

This is a fungal disease that is occasionally caused by bacteria that penetrate the leaf and kill its tissue. Its symptoms include shades and powdery, whitish growth on the leaf surface; it's most common during the summer, and it can be controlled by removing all the infected leaves and use of fungicides.

White Mold

This is caused by the fungus that sleeps through winter in the soil; the fungus infects the plant stem that touches the moist soil. It is characterized by white mold that collapses the infected tissue by girdling it. It can be prevented by staking flexible stem to sustain the plant, using the right spacing between the plants to allow for air circulation, and avoiding damp conditions.

Benefits of Perennials

Unlike most annual plants, perennials cannot be fully relied on for daily feeding needs. Nevertheless, perennials are of great importance, especially in permaculture. Some of the benefits of perennials are:

Improvement of the Soil Structure

Because they live in the soil for many years, perennial flowers' roots improve the soil structure. Their extensive roots create soil spaces, allowing water to penetrate it, and help soil aerate. This benefits the microorganisms, which decomposes the organic matter, effectively releasing the nutrients to the soil.

Enriching the Soil with Nutrients

As we have already talked, perennials have deeper roots than annuals. With their deep roots, they can access nutrients found in the soils and bring them to the surface; thanks to this, even the other plants, as the annuals that otherwise would not get there, can access more air.

They Act as Ground Covers

By providing a ground cover, perennials maintain the soil moisture by preventing evaporation. This helps maintain the soil structure and avoid soil erosion from wind or water after heavy rain.

They are Easily Propagated

Perennials can be propagated easier than annuals through stem cuttings and rootstocks, because the firsts are stronger and, often, bigger than the seconds. Cuttings can be made from one perennial flower and planted in a whole garden; then, you can wait for the flowers to bloom and uproot them to get rootstocks.

Perennials are many varieties

With many varieties of perennials, you can maintain your garden color throughout the seasons, and you can also have productive seasons throughout the year; the most important step is that you make sure to plant perennials in the right period.

Chapter 8: How to create structure's for landscaping

Garden Planning and Designing

We are at the practical steps of this guide, now. Seeing you on the practical, could make you feel a bit uncomfortable, due to the fear to make wrong: your garden could grow wild and overgrown or bleak and unimaginative, and that couldn't sound very comforting. However, be happy and relaxed: in whatever current condition is your garden, it can be turned into your ideal outdoor setting with a bit of motivation, thinking and preparation. Let's look at the practical steps together, to understand the real key to creating the perfect landscape: **build for one purpose.**

What Sort of Outdoor Garden Do You Want?

The very first step is deciding what you plan to do at the greenhouse: it'll help you allocate space better. Are you sure how many spaces should be created? Have you divided your garden into zones? Do you want to create a relaxing area? Do you want to create mostly a beautiful entrance? Ask yourself if you really could create all of areas in your project. For instance, people often don't want to build a long rest as children need room to run around; that does not just mean choosing one priority according to your desires, but also for the whole family. Remember, then, to consider everybody's needs carefully; the following questions can help you to do this.

- Will this fit in for the kids?
- Do you want a space to drink and eat with your friends?
- Do you want a barbecue area?
- Do you need a space for your pets to run around?
- Do you want to create a specific area for your pets?
- Does your wife/husband want to create a space in which to spent time reading or relaxing?
- Does someone want to make growing plants to have fresh fruits and vegetables?

First Get Inspired

Seeking a bit of inspiration from which to decide on your backyard is crucial. There are innumerable options to do it, and you could select either one type you prefer or a mix of a couple. You can get inspiration getting out and seeing your neighbor's gardens, or searching on the web, or by:

- Supermarket catalogs, magazine articles and collections, that could be a nature guide or a tale highlighting your favorite celebrities' garden.
- Exploring outdoor environments: trips to stunning homes and romantic vacation places, common beaches, mates, and loved one's garden; take a peek at what you want. Take pictures (where

necessary) and create a potentials list. You may not be able to reproduce these designs in your yard, but at this early point, nothing is off-limits.

Select the Visual of your Garden

Always double check the garden look you have decided, because it should help you refine what you're projecting; you may have chosen more than one color, or you may have chosen two or three different themes. Checking more than one times, you might consider that two colors don't suit together, or even styles contrast together. Instead, maybe you could choose to keep all of them in your garden, or find that you've got a large garden that fits more than one style. Interestingly, the clean lines of the asymmetrical formal garden may be restful on the eye (since the brain does not have to work hard to interpret the image), and you might consider asymmetric style if you really want the garden to look wider.

Creation of a Landscape Layout

Choose a piece of paper and draw a diagram of your garden using a measuring tape to precisely quantify all of your garden's critical

dimensions and components, including any features or dots defined. Don't forget to identify the position of any pipes or cables; you could try to avoid them while landscaping, but have to recognize where they are going to be and make them available. You'll also want to pick up a tracker to monitor your yard's rise and decline, too. Including everything you need to remember and wisely bid your time will hopefully help you from making any expensive errors later on.

Your Garden Knowledge

Local knowledge of weather and the climate: The healthiest gardens include interacting with the native environment and using plants that will naturally thrive there. Even if you live in an especially adverse place (whether open and windy or with sea breezes around the coast), there are plenty you might do to make your landscape more appropriate for a range of plants! However, if you're foreign to a region, it can be difficult to understand those local trends; in this case, get friends in your neighborhood and asked them about this.

Knowledge about the soil: Strong soil is essential for good and healthy plants. These are several forms from the worst to best: loams, stone, dirt, straw, silt, and topsoil. Identifying what kind of soil you have will help you know which plants you're going to develop and how well they will survive after planting. This might also be important for landscaping projects since some are much harder to work with than others.

Consider a part of your garden*:* What way do you face in your garden? To the south, to the north, east, and west? Understand the direction and 'aspect' will allow you to find out where you want everything to go; for example, there's little interest in getting a decked space in the shadiest part of the garden to appreciate the sunlight! Sketch the light's path onto your plan, so you'll see where the shades fall off. Moreover, check out microclimates: all gardens have a different variety of bio-climates defined by alternation of sunlight and shade, presence of water and animals.

Continue Carrying Out the New Landscape Scheme

Draw more than one paper for the initial design to accommodate the newest improvements: looking at them together allows you to choose the best things of all of them! Mess with dimensions and forms to see the best result; begin with several buildings, structures, and wide parts of the garden (like the water features). This will let you see what space you have and how the rest of the greenhouse can be affected. Look for equilibrium between all-beds, pounds, relaxing area, playgrounds for children, and more. Let due time to all sections to avoid one part of the garden become busy while others remain too empty. Even a small building or tree could swamp a tiny area, while putting too small items in larger areas leaves spaces too empty.

Test the Rule and Talk With Neighbors

Planning laws vary from region to region, but typically very strict limits are imposed on what can be achieved in protected areas with the buildings or property listed, which involves their gardens. Some new buildings are prone to these limitations, so it is, therefore, worth checking with the local authority's planning department to ensure that what you want to build is acceptable. Even though you'll not do a too complex project, it's worth sitting down with your zone expert and control every aspect and all the implications you can face. You can also talk with your neighbors: they could be already efforted with these rules, and they can suggest to you what you can do or not in your project.

Chapter 9: Landscaping for Entry

How to Install a Beautiful Walkway

Creating a classic landscaping design in the front yard is easy cheap but takes a bit of work. First of all, you have to choose if the pathway line will be symmetric or asymmetric; then you have to choose the color of the material. Depending on the material using and the place of the walkway, your garden look could change completely!

To avoid a result that doesn't satisfy you, carefully choose the bricks or tiles; after buying them, though, look at the material's really color bring it in sunlight, because the color could be different a little into the shop, but you will pose it outdoor! For example: if your house is white and you want to make a grey walkway, finding a dark grey slab that matches the house white could create a beautiful effect; the same slabs, though, could become too dark in a rainy area, due to the constant presence of clouds. To avoid a lack of aesthetic value alongside the entry walk, remember that an extended lawn view and some beautiful plants or items offer a particularly refreshing view. The path to the front door can also be designed to take advantage of differing views. It's not necessary for the walk to be straight in terms of line; even if the house door is in front of the gate in a straight one, you can create two forks, or add one or two turns add excitement and encourage you to change the view of the front doorway.

Note, however, if you want the path to curve, it should have some physical cause, like rocks or patios; avoid aimless curves, as they can look unnatural and visually unappealing.

Steps to create a Walkway

#Step 1: Select the future walkway place

Using a paint or sticks, carefully mark the area where you want to create the walkway. Remove any dirty and sod; if there are old tiles there, remove them.

 # Step 2: Find the materials

Make sure to have all you need. I suggest you choose the color of the Joint Sand related to the tiles. If you live in a rainy area, avoid slippery materials. This is a shortlist of the essential materials.

Materials:

- Pavers base panels
- Joining Sand
- Landscape Stakes (optional)
- Paver
- Non-woven fabric
- Paving
- Builder's Sand
- Joining Sand

Tools:

- Plate compactor
- Hand tamper
- Shovel
- Rubber mallet
- Stake for tiles
- Tiles cutter
- Garden rake
- Tape measure
- Level

#Step 3: Remove the soil and create your first layer

The depth level of the excavation depends on the paver thickness

1. Using a shovel, dig a 5" deep base *plus the thickness of the flagstone or brick* (example: if the tile thickness is 1", you have to dig a layer 5+1" deep)
2. Level the bottom using a rake and a plate compactor (control by a level)
3. Put a non-woven fabric on all of the layer bottom (this is optional, but putting the landscape fabric prevent weed formation)
4. Fill the layer with the gravel up to the 4" deep (example: if the tile thickness is 1" and your layer is 6" deep, you must put a 4" layer of gravel, to remain with 2" free). Spread it by plate compactor.
5. Fill the remained 1" deep layer with builder's sand. Spread it by a plate compactor. You should remain only with the tile thickness deep.
6. When your ground is ready and solid, remove the dusty or residues.

Step 4: Create your walkway

1. Cut your tiles by a tiles cutter or making small holes with the drill along the tile's line you want to cut
2. Place the stones/tiles in area, adding a bit of builder's sand on each tile back. Each tile must distance 1" from each other. Use a level to check the tiles are parallel to the ground.
3. Put the Joining Sand in every space between every tile to block them.
4. Top the pathway with more builder's Sand

#Step 5: Enjoy your pathway!

1. Clean your tiles from the sand, before it dries; you can use a piece of wet cotton fabric.
2. Congratulations! You created a beautiful walkway!

Driveway

The driveway's primary purpose is to give car parking space. The minimum usable width is **10 ft.** for a single-car drive, but you could need to expand the parking zone more. If the driveway is also working as the walk from the road and to the front door, **the driveway must be broadened by 3 ft.** or more. Without the additional distance, if a car is pulled up at the drive, there is no space for walking, and this could pressure people to walk alongside the slim edge of the car or stride onto the nearby lawn or plant area. Expansion of the drive area will make it easy for people to walk comfortably.

There are three important components to the construction of the driveway:

- Giving a secure approach
- Leading people through the landscape
- Impacting their view

In some houses entrance walks are badly constructed and therefore don't work effectively: among the most frequent issues is a too little restricted entry walk. Indeed, walkways are usually 3 ft wide, which compels people to walk one at a time; they should be no less than 4 ft wide to manage two people walking side by side. For wheelchair access, it should at least be 5 ft. wider. The overgrown is one related issue: shrubs grown too near the walk can decrease the width available and will eventually end up enveloping the walk. Another concern is the entry walk position: in a large garden, the plant placement may and should prompt the eye towards the entry direction, and then on the walkway: if it is too asymmetric could be worsen the garden in general, and if it has too curves you could lengthen the arrive at the house door. If the garden is small, the walkway's corrected place is next to the driveway, but there will be less attention to the walkway, even if it is more colorful.

The differences between Driveway and Pathway

The pathway is thinner than the driveway, obviously, but you must keep in mind this concept because people need to create both a driveway and pathway in most cases. You always have to add a walkway to your project, and it could be created with several materials: stones, slate, bricks, mosaic, or simply gravel. Every type of pathway you'll choose could be built in the same way, as I have already explained. The driveway is only "a larger walkway": the building is the same, but the size is different! Keep in mind the measurement above, but mostly make sure these could be done in your project. You could make a different driveway from the pathway using different materials or making one of these higher than the other. If there isn't space for both in your garden, but you live in a central area, I suggest you choose to create a driveway instead pathway, to avoid parking difficulties; you could create an intimate area in your backyard, where stay out with your friends. However, if you live in a not busy area, where you can park your car without problems, I suggest you create a more lovely and decorated pathway, if you have to choose.

Area for greeting

Usually, the entry walk comes to an end in front of the front door and often reaches a small-scaled concrete slab that acts as an entrance or area for greeting outside; you have to make this space large for two people minimum. Often in some houses, the slabs are so narrow that it makes it uncomfortable for people to step on it, and to enter into the house, they must get a step away from the door to avoid getting struck by it!

Think about expanding that paving area to assist two or three persons comfortably. Providing some form of extra protection from elements is also beneficial; the overhead protection prevents you from getting soaked in the rain. You can also create a sensation of semi-privacy at the entry by planting alongside some high plants or structures; it may give a feeling of enclosure. Be mindful of plant sizes and their positioning to avoid covering the front door from the road.

Landscape accents

Accent components that include mostly specimen plants serve as focal points to catch the viewer's attention. Therefore, they should be regarded

as adornments and should be used limited; an adornment that includes sundials, birdbaths, gazing balls, and obelisks tends to divert attention and diminishes the front yard's unity as well as balance. If you fancy decorative elements, place them in the private backyard area. Decorative plants can either be trees or shrubs, which serve as focal points due to their exceptional ornamental features; these plants attract attention to themselves by their very nature. One of the trouble with placing a specimen plant in your front yard is that it becomes the main focal point easily, diverting attention from the door at the front; to avoid this, therefore, specimen plants should be placed close to the door to naturally lead the viewer's attention from the plant to the door. In the front garden, consider using only one specimen tree; too close trees will compete with each other and with the house. Try to pick a non-overly dominant plant: a shrub with spring flowers or a small tree would be a great choice.

Front-Yard Landscaping Ideas

If you want only a cheerful and lovely front-yard full of Filipino Lilies and Orchids, then we will make our way back a bit. There are several ways to create a beautiful show, even if you have limited room and money; however, when it comes to landscaping the front yard, you wouldn't have to embrace mediocrity. Once you've learned some landscaping tips, you'll be on your way to building a stunning front yard at a limited budget.

Here are four cheap solutions for front yard landscaping renovations:

Install a Stone Walkway

This classic landscaping design is surprisingly cheap at the front yard and takes only a bit of work. Steppingstones may be found differently: you can have stones in your garden and fill your pathway with them and concrete or buy stones in a landscaping hardware shop.

Replace the Stones and Pebbles

In your front yard, another gritty idea is to pave the whole front yard with a combination of pebbles, gravel, and shrubs. Over the year, you'll save on all kinds of maintenance costs, such as drainage and sodding; and with fewer lawns to cut per week, you'll have plenty of free time to focus on those landscaping projects in the backyard.

Low-Cost Gravel Path

A gravel path is extremely budget-friendly and is a great idea for the front yard, particularly if you have very little foliage in these areas of high passage. The estimated cost of a 100-foot gravel path is around $650; you might need to add another shovel of gravel, but the end product would be worth it altogether.

Small Tree Planted Opposite Your Yard

A lone tree on a tiny front yard is a perfect focal point, moreover, if it is full of foliage, it can provide your home with a lot of shade and potentially reduce your air conditioning costs up to 30%. Take the time to consider this aspect in your landscaping designs at the front yard.

Chapter 10: Landscaping for open spaces

For those who enjoy entertaining guests, a social garden design is ideal, because it considers privacy above all else. The best way to provide such privacy for yourself, your family, and your guests is to plant trees and plants called "climbers" to form a natural screen. If you opt for trees, be sure to avoid planting them too close to your house or your neighbors' home or because the roots can, with time, damage your (or their) foundation. Alternatively, you can place trees at the end of the garden area to form a screen that does not hinder the view you have from your home. Once you have established your privacy, you need to create a seating area. If you don't have time, you might create a part of the area and build the rest in the future. First of all, you can create a very sleek paving area, customized to your garden theme or tastes, and a gazebo to shade during the summer. Weatherproof furniture is an important component; if you want to buy outdoor furniture, you have to plan where it will be placed and forecast the amount of shade and sunlight a specific garden area receives. You will have to keep track of where the sun falls

throughout the day and where the warmth will be. For example, when people dining they tend to prefer shade; if your yard is sunny most of the time with no naturally shaded area, you will need to plant something that creates shade, like a row of tall bushes which form a screen, and you can place your outdoor dining furniture under this screen.

Be practical and realistic about the design; if you want to include a dining

area, you might not have room to include a garden shed. This means that your gardening tools will need a new home. In such cases, try to think practically: use seats or design a table that has a lid on top and doubles as a tabletop workbench. This allows you a place to store your garden tools discreetly while you are entertaining. When it comes to seating, look for comfort no matter the design you want and invest money in weatherproof seat cushions: guests will want someplace soft to sit and relax when you bring them outside! Buy good quality seat cushions means both extending your outdoor furniture's longevity and saving time, throwing easily them in the wash if they get too dirty. If you decide to have an outdoor deck, one that is raised, you will need to soften the edges visually; this does not mean you have to change the outdoor deck design, but rather, leave the deck protruding and cover the borders with different plants. If you can, you could plant close the social area some local scented herbs or fresh herbs: they will visually soften the social garden design; moreover, they smell great and if you are cooking outside, you can pick one or two fresh herbs to sprinkle on top of your dishes! As a finishing touch to your social garden design, you could add trellises around your dining area. that offer a very coordinated and neat appearance. They are also easier amended than old fences. I suggest you leave scented climbing plants, like Jasmine, to grow up on the trellis: this not only gives you an aesthetically appealing private escape but also offers a wonderful aroma.

Fountains and Waterworks

A sure way to add interest in every garden and to mimic the scenes in nature is to have a working waterworks system. You can create fountains of any size and type: with statues spouting water into a pool, mini waterfalls, or simulated streams which aside from being visually attractive, give off that gentle soothing sound of rushing water. You could draw water from an underground spring or river by building a well. Aside from being a possible water source, fountains could be a thing of beauty as well. Fountains and water bodies could be an essential component of landscaping: they have a soothing effect on the psychology of a person. and increase the aesthetic value of your landscape. Water, through its property of reflectivity, can be used to create magic. Not all fountains and water bodies cannot be created in all sites due to the eventual scarcity of water. To remove this doubt, you should control if the groundwater is approximately at a depth of 300' - 350' maximum below the ground level in your garden.

Ponds and Bridges

One way of getting close to nature is to create habitats for living creatures. One of the most commonly made is a fishpond: it is a great way to house your aquatic animal friends, creating little spots of attractive landscaping.

If the pond (or pool) is big enough, one may even put in a bridge to better view and feed the fishes, and get you from one side to the other. Having ponds is a good way of nourishing aquatic flora and fauna as well. You can have water lilies or lotuses to spruce up the surface of the pond or pool beautifully.

Landscaping for relaxing spaces

There are times when we all need a break from the stresses of the world. You can create an avenue of escape by placing little quiet nooks for peace and meditation right in your own garden or yard. You can put in benches, chairs, pillows, mats, rugs, or even a hammock or day bed to add comfort; bamboo fountains, meditating stones, and crystals could be incorporated into the design for an extra calming effect. Screens and hedges can be strategically positioned for optimum privacy and seclusion. You can put an adjustable shade on the patio to use it during both dry and wet weather, while providing you with ample space to be alone. A Zen oasis can be created with a minimalist theme; it is simple to build and there are fewer plants to be maintained, in keeping with the clean line's concept.

Where do you could create the relaxing area?

If you have enough space, you can create a special area in a remote angle of your garden: enclose it with edges or trees, and place there a gazebo to repair yourself from bad weather or sun. You could create a little spa area, installing a hydromassage, or a little pool with chromotheraphy. If you have less space, you could create your perfect relaxing area in the backyard: this part, normally, is the quietest.

Backyard Landscaping

If you are fortunate enough to have a backyard, you already have the beginnings of what could soon be the most relaxing area of your home. After a long work week, all people desire a place to go where it is peaceful and restful; with the proper planning for backyard landscaping ideas, your backyard could be this retreat. We will discuss several ideas for backyard landscaping.

Flowers, Trees, and other Plants

One of the best ways to create your own personal paradise is to create a garden of "Eden" in your backyard by planting your favorite types of trees, especially fruit trees and by other scented plants. If you plant according to the right blooming, the more flowers/plants you put in it, the more colors you will enjoy. When it comes to creating a spectacular garden, there are many types of gardens to choose from: many of them are simple and inexpensive to create. A rock garden is one of the easiest gardens to create: all you need are plenty of rocks, plenty of your favorite flowers, a little time, and some imagination.

Water Features

Adding water features to your backyard is one of the best methods of backyard landscaping. There are many different water features on the market, but you can create your own water feature. Whether you purchase a water feature or create your own, they are simple and inexpensive to create, and it adds beauty to your backyard instantaneously; there is nothing more relaxing than listening to the sound of running water.

Gazebos

Many people make their backyard more livable adding a gazebo; some of these are inexpensive and can be constructed by the homeowner in most cases. A gazebo creates a comfortable place to relax or have cookouts and other family gatherings; you can also decorate your gazebo with flowers, climbing plants and add furniture to create an awesome sitting area.

Chapter 11: Time and budget for DIY Landscaping

To sum up the previous chapters, we look at the main concepts to keep in mind to create a great landscape gardening:

1) Assure you have a plan in mind when planning your garden landscape: you should also consider forecast on the height and width of the trees or plants you plan to plant in your garden, to avoid turn it into a mix of unmanageable views and paths.
2) Assure to understand the needs of the plants you'll buy, if they are annuals, perennials, and need sun or shade; the way the garden receives sun and shade throughout the day can change at maturity of your landscape project, and some sunlight-friendly plants could end up in the shade. Remember to seed new sprouts according to their blooming period, to always have a colorful garden.
3) Consider if the curb will bring value to your garden landscape design. Keep in mind that the backyard might be where you will more often hanging out, but the rest of the world will always see the front yard garden design! So, you could opt for an inexpensive landscape design following the natural curves in your garden; nature doesn't just work in straight lines! This form of landscaping will improve your garden's look appeal, adding value to your home. Don't forget the importance of pathway: if you can, it is good to create both driveway and pathway, but if you can't, you can create a driveway 3-4 ft larger to allow people to reach house door.

4) When designing your garden landscape, account should be taken of the family's future needs. If you have kids, plan your garden with them and keep in mind their needs; if you have pets, you could create space to allow them to run; in every case, each member of the family could make different use of the garden, and you should add the most of them in your landscape project.
5) Lighting, both natural and artificial, is among the most overlooked elements of landscape design. In every garden, the lighting plays a vital role: garden illumination sets the atmosphere and allows people to use gardens during daytime and at night. Have a functional lighting system is also fundamental to have more safety in general. Irrigation is another vital aspect, whether artificial or natural, because plants need the right water quantity. To have lasting landscaping, you must pay attention to the irrigation system.
6) When you design your garden landscape, make sure that it is built around your personality, preferences and maintenance needs; if you really like designing an oriental garden, you will not plant roses, as well as, if you like your local garden style, you will not opt to plants tropical elements. The future maintenance of your landscape design should be a major decision: if you have a little time, you will not opt for complex maintenance. If you don't have the time or the maintenance ability, but you will create a too complex project, maybe your landscape design could fail.

Your garden landscape design doesn't have to be costly necessarily; you only have to make sure you are cost-realistic. It is very easy to misjudge the cost of landscaping, especially if you hire contractors. You have to plan a realistic budget for your garden and following there are some tips that will help you do it.

Designing on a budget

Setting your budget is one of the most important steps. However, you decide to pay for this new venture, whether it be with credit cards, cash, or financing, you need to have a reasonable budget set aside for it. Unfortunately, most people believe in creating a super landscaping project with 100$. To avoid this, make sure that you do the right research when setting a budget. Search the price of all items you wish, and make a list:

- Stones, slate, gravel, concrete, bricks, topsoil, rocks;
- Shovel, trowel, garden gloves, vases, fences, mulch, fertilizer, gardening tools;
- Plants, seeds, flowers, little trees, supports for plants;
- Blocks of wood, trellis, cushions, benches, tables, barbecues, playground;
- Fountains, cables, pipes, irrigation system, lights, sculptures, bird baths;

When you found every price, you could start looking for them on sale; however, do not expect Tiffany products at discount prices. Set how much you want to add maximum, where you want to add it (for example, to create a better one area instead of another), and write it. If you know you can only afford to add a retaining wall for now, then set the budget as such; if you prefer to have the patio first, then plan accordingly. Never get in over your plan: you don't have to go into massive debt to get the whole package! You can prioritize, set the proper budget, and get what you want. If you can afford one thing or don't find any that satisfies you, you can build this tomorrow!

When deciding on a budget, obviously, there are many factors, but you have to prioritize something. Consider everything you want to have done, write it down and go over the list. What do you must do first of all? What can wait until you save up some more? Have you added too many items to your list? Asking yourself this question, put your answers on paper, visualize the changes, and start from there. When you can see your goals on paper, your thought process becomes a lot clearer than just going over it in your head; it gives you a more tangible element to look at.

Remember! At the design stage, it's very important NOT to think about your budget; If you worry too much whilst designing, it will prevent you from coming up with anything good. You must think about the budget only after you have decided what you want to create in your garden, to do realistic your project. Divide the first creative part from the second one, more logical and rational.

Whilst your budget will affect the type of patio you have and the materials you can use, there are ways you can get the look you want more affordably. At the design stage, it's very important NOT to think about your budget.

Decide Your Budget Options

As beautiful and long lasting as precision cut and finished natural stone paving is, it could be too expensive; there are cheaper materials in the short term, as reclaimed paving, concrete, and basic natural stone.

If you fell in love with LED lighting, but the budget won't allow you to build the system as you want right now, then put in some ducting pipes under the patio for an electric cable to insert through at a later date. The same thing can be done with raised planters and built-in seating: they don't necessarily have to be built simultaneously as the patio. Some things are better done in one go, though; create the foundation should be done first, even if you don't have the budget for all structures. For example, if you want to build two walls, but you have a budget only for one, you should dig the foundations for all of them, creating immediately one wall and cover the other wall's foundations with materials you could remove easily in the future; doing this, you avoid to destroy a part of your garden by excavation and bringing machinery again. Indeed, bringing machinery on-site to dig out all footings (even the future ones) or do clearance is much more cost effective to do it one hit; also, you will not want to have heavy machinery going over your lovely news patio and lawn at a later date!

Hiring a Contractor

If you cannot do the work yourself, get a contractor that you can trust. Ask him to give you a quote for building the entire garden and tell him you want to do it in phases, if it is what you really want to do. Talk to him about your budget and understand if he can do for you. Usually, contractors try to do as much as is possible because if they don't do well with phase one, they know then you won't call them back to do therest. However, in any case, if you find a good contractor, ask him to sign an agreement about the work times, the budget limit, and the unexpected accidents.

Tips to create a friendly-budget landscape

Considering enhancing your **backyard** but worried about what it can cost? No problems! There are heaps of cheap landscaping design elements you could create or change to improve your garden look. Check these budget-friendly ideas.

Use of Mulching Alternatives

Mulching is a time and energy saver because it reduces the amount of water and requires mowing in the garden; however, mulching itself can be expensive. That's why having a cheap mulch option for the project at the backyard is one of the better options. Here is a list of cheaper mulching substitute:

Grass Cuttings: The very next moment you mow, the cuttings and gains could be put on the flower bed and raked up.

Leaves: crushed leaves provide your plants with a nice, inexpensive replacement mulch and also fertilizer.

Wood Cones: A replacement for mulch relatively low maintenance, durable, and quick to scatter.

Compost: Since you've just made your first compost tank, you can use it in all of the garden. Only beware of not covering it too thickly, since so much will heat up and destroy your plants.

Newspaper: Let your plants take care of the humorous Sunday papers you've bought: spread between four to six pages on the ground, spray softly, and cover with topsoil before planting.

Sand: Sand mulch is not suitable for all flowers, but the weeding and maintenance costs will be great in the long term if used correctly.

Former Tires Reuse

Tires are voluminous and can be hard to eliminate because many waste delivery trucks do not allow them. Why not put them back in your yard for good use? Here are a couple of cheap ways to landscape your yard using tires:

- For a robust and rustic ottoman patio, cover with a pillow or corded patio enclosures.
- Lined and installed tires to produce ornamental planters.
- Build a hanging planter by filling one half of it with soil and adding it to a wall or fence.
- Create a groundbreaking indoor pool with a rim in the backyard.
- Give your child a nice place to have fun with a reused tire climber.

Plant Upside-Down

Do you love gardening but have little space or money to do it? There could be a clear solution in view. Vertical planting utilizes vertical space specifically placed for plant growth; the vertical gardens are a perfect starting point when you're looking for a budget for tiny landscaping projects in the backyard. Not only they make the most of limited resources, but they can also be inexpensive, particularly if you're using recycled materials such as old plastic water bottles. Following are the DIY planting ideas:

- You can create a rustic vertical garden on front porch using a wooden staircase, terracotta pots, and some cord.
- Clean old bottles of paint, fill them with soil, and bring them together to create a vertical herb garden.

- To create a succulent vertical greenhouse, using a photo frame or a durable, unused footwear organizer.

- Use pot hangers and wooden screws to transform your fence into a vertical garden.

Apply a Spray-On Paint

Often what's needed is to add some hue to make a landscape glow. This can be as easy as painting plantings to give the garden a more modern feel, or adding a new coat of paint to the wood, or sheet metal chairs. Reuse the leftover paint from previous ventures to save still more on your backyard flower bed, rather than purchasing fresh colors. A small splash of color gives instantaneously another look to your garden, even if it is inexpensive! It may also be added plants' vases, put on balconies, gazeboes, or entry doors.

Change the place

You can quickly transform your backyard from plants that repel pests into a beautiful and usable space changing the place of vases' plants, flower beds, or putting some little plants into a full topsoil wheelbarrow; you can also use some of terracotta planters.

Creating an Open-Air Chimney

There's no easier way to get the kids around a fire pit. Yet you don't have to pay for a builder to bring one up: you can build your own backyard campfire station in just a few minutes, with one ride to the home improvement store. You can get some rocks out from some other garden job; a rocks pyre is a perfect place to make a campfire with your kids.

Planting a Tree

One of the simplest -and least expensive- tasks of any landscaping project is tree planting; cultivating plants that grow slowly in your yard, with excellent preparation, will theoretically save you money in the long run. Indeed, all you need is just a few digging devices, every mulch, and the tree.

Using Cheaper Light Beacons

Cheap outdoor light bulbs are a favorite for backyard landscaping. In a chilling summer, the light and the atmospheric glow will bright every patio they meet. White sparkle lighting costs about $6/piece, or you can even pick up a set of white horizon lights for around $9 for a more glamorous look. While globe light clusters are slightly more costly, they are usually more robust than sparkle light, and quickly substitute the bulbs.

Buy (or Make) Low-Cost Seats

If you have completed your budget landscaping programs, remember that it doesn't exist only the local home furnishings shop: you can easily look for lower-prices for the same furniture online, or make them yourself.

Chapter 12: Landscaping elements and low wall

Wall Gardening Flowerbed

To create this, you will have to set some hardwood or concrete bars on your wall, horizontally, "to create a terracing". All of the bars must be fixed at the same high. When you've fixed the bars, set at the top of all a wood panel covering all the wall length. Then, start to cover the frontal part of your new "wall"; from the ground up to 1ft higher than the bars, you put the bricks, in column. Once your tray is filled with topsoil and your seedlings are planted, you could have something like the image above. Water just the topmost columns. These types of flowerbeds can be more beautiful in your garden.

Patios

For your social garden design, if you are going to host summer outdoor cookouts or parties, you might consider incorporating the patio for additional accessibility and functionality. Figure out what you want the patio to be used for, and that will help you figure out the size. **A small space which is roughly 8' x 8' is perfect if you just want to cook but not necessarily seat all of your guests on the patio.**

There are many shapes available, including rectangular and square shapes for attractive patio designs. Create a square paving is obviously the more traditional route. To create your small patio you can use bricks, tiles, or landscaping stones; these are perfect if you plan on having any type of seating area and need a level surface on which to place yourfurniture.

Concerning the materials available for your patio, **concrete** is durable and easily customizable, because you can change its color before you mix it; however, it can only be poured in good weather and can beexpensive. **Paving stones** could be a more attractive option that is reasonably priced, but you have to prepare the area by making it level to use paving stones.

Bricks are great because of the starting performance and variety of color options; the only downside with brick is that the site, much like paving stones, has to be prepared ahead of time so that each brick fit snugly with those bricks around it. **Gravel** could be another great choice available in multiple sizes, styles, and colors; it's very affordable, and if your patio is being used for dining, gravel will provide a sturdy surface for your furniture.

If you already have a patio, you can decorate the area with a pergola or a gazebo.

Steps to create your first Patio

#Step 1: Draw your project on your project sheet

Take your house planimetry and start drawing the space/spaces in which you would create your patio. When you are sure where you want to build it, add a draw to your project sheet. Make the drawing to scale, checking the real measurements on your garden, to visualize it better (possibly with the help of an architect or surveyor).

#Step 2: Imagine your patio!

If you are uncertain about the patio look, you can answer these questions:

- Do you want an open patio or a close area?
- If your patio is adjacent to the house, from which door do you want to access the patio?
- Will you need stairs to access to your future patio?
- Do you want to create a ground-level patio or a raised one?
- In which place do you want to put the furniture (as a barbecue, chairs, table…)?
- Do your kids will be able to reach patio safely?
- Do you want to add a pergola or gazebo to your patio?
- What paving should be the most perfect to your patio?
- Do you want to lighten your patio?
- What type of view you want to see from it?

Remember: It is your first project! I suggest you avoid create more than one level in your patio: if you want to create a raised patio, it is fantastic, but to make easier your first realize, you should create one level, which you access via the stairs. Moreover, creating too many levels would risk being dangerous for children or the elderly, especially if the patio is tiny and you want a table on it! If you create the stairs to access your patio, you should secure them by making a railing or balustrade to prevent people from falling!
The balustrades break the visual impact; for example, if you have a large garden, which you access via the patio with a balustrade, this will catch the eye of everyone who looks at your garden. Therefore, it is important that the balustrade is aesthetically beautiful and with materials related to your patio: if you have a wooden floor on the patio, you can build a lighter color wooden balustrade, or can create a transparent one.

#Step 4: Create your patio

What you'll need

- Stakes or paint
- Spade
- Garden hoses
- Landscape fabric
- Gravel
- Builder's sand
- Flagstones, bricks, or pavers
- Plate compactor
- Jointing Sand

1. Mark your patio border by stakes or paint. Remove the sod.
2. If there are old tiles or rocks in your area, remove them.
3. Excavate a 5-inch-deep base *plus the thickness of the tile, brick, or flagstone* using a shovel (for example if your tile's thickness is 1", you will dig a 5+1" deep).
4. Level the bottom by a rake and spread it with plate compactor.
5. Put the sheet of non-woven fabric on the soil bottom (is an optional step but putting the landscape fabric prevent weed formation).
6. Fill the layer with the gravel up to the 4" deep (example: if the tile thickness is 1" and your layer is 6" deep, you must put a 4" layer of

gravel, to remain with 2" free). Spread it by plate compactor.

7. Fill the remained 1" deep layer with builder's sand. Spread it by a plate compactor. You should remain only with the tile thickness deep.
8. When your soil is ready and solid, remove the dusty or residues, using a broom.
9. Cut your tiles by a tiles cutter or making small holes with the drill along the tile's line you want to cut
10. Place the flagstones/bricks/tiles in area, adding a bit of builder's sand on each tile back. Each tile must distance 1" from each other. Use a level to check the tiles are parallel to the ground.
11. Put the Joining Sand in every space between every tile to block them.
12. Top your patio with more builder's sand.

 # Step 5: Enjoy your patio!

13. Clean your patio from the sand before it dries using a cotton cloth wet.
14. Congratulations! You can add the furniture to your patio!

Tips to create your first patio

- You can add a pergola o gazebo to your patio to create relaxing shade. You can easily build the structure with wood or stainless steel and complete the pergola with adding a color cloth on the top. Alternatively, you can fix wattle panels on the top and add linen curtains on the sides, which creates a more romantic vibe.
- Complete your patio with a necessary for an outdoor dinner: a table, some chairs and a barbecue will fill your summer evenings with friends and fun!
- Play with the lights: when the sun goes down, it is nice to see a patio lit up by warm lights. Put some outdoor spotlights; you can find them

with integrated solar panels. If your patio is close to the house wall or garden border, you can also apply some wall lights.

- Use basic geometric shapes as rectangular or square; if you want to create a circular patio, buy a pre-formed pavement; to level each of tiles, making them a perfect circle, is really complex even for advanced landscapers! I suggest avoiding using hexagonal or octagonal shapes.

Arbors

In your beautiful project, you can also create rooms with a view using vines, canopies, and pergolas as the "walls" and "roof" of your outdoor room to hide you from the harsh glare of the sun with these little shelters. Plants can be used to create seemingly "living" walls that offer enough coverage for privacy and seclusion. They only must have a stable structure to grow on. You can create little spaces with intimate seating; it could be an ideal setting for romantic dinners and dates! Roses can be grown on an arbor to form a natural roof that is all at once functional, beautiful, and sweet-smelling. The climber plants could be added to a pergola or gazebo to create a relaxing shade and a more vibrant atmosphere.

Vertical Garden

You can go for one hundred styles of gardening; choose your favorite and, enjoy it! As a beginner, let us choose one from the styles below.

<u>To create your Vertical Garden, you will need specific materials:</u>

- A big panel of hardwood;
- A Cardboard panel (must have the same measurements of hardwood panel);
- Trellis or poles (optional);
- Heavy duty weed mat;
- Specific Vertical Garden PVC mat;
- Star pickets or 8" screws;
- Sifted compost; river sand, coco peat and topsoil;
- Your plant;
- Little vases (optional);

Create a Vertical Garden Step to Step:

1) Make a frame on your wall by woods using the hardwood panel; fixed it very well!
2) Cover its right and left with the heavy duty weed mat;
3) Cover the front of hardwood panel with the specific PVC mat;

4) Cut holes on the cardboard panel; each of the holes will have to contain a PVC pocket, then you must make the holes at the same high to the pockets. I suggest you make circular holes 4-5" diameter minimum;
5) Fix the Cardboard panel to the hardwood one using 8" screw or star pickets; the hardwood and the cardboard should be distanced * 5-6" from each other;
6) Pull out each pocket from the holes, and put your plant very carefully into each of the pockets;
7) Put the mix of sifted compost, river sand, coco peat, and topsoil into them;
8) Water it: make it all wet;
9) Gradually your plants will grow!

Depending on where you place your Vertical Garden and the sunlight/shade it receives, you can grow plants such as Thyme, Oregano, Rosemary, Petunia, Daisies, Orchid, Strawberries and so on.

How to install a little wall

For your first project, I suggest you build only division walls, high up to **5ft maximum**; if you want to create higher walls, or make retaining walls, or want to create a wall on a knoll, you should find a good contractor,

because it could be necessary put some irons inside the bricks and the concrete. To reinforce the concrete, you have to put in the first compact hardcore layer some irons 10" height over the ground (if the bricks are closed) or 15" height over the ground (if the bricks are open).

#Step 1: Decide the place, the style and find the materials

After you have analyzed where you want to build the wall, mark the ground with your wall's width and length using paint or sticks. You can choose whichever style for you wall: you could create a **Mortared Stonewall** or a **Brick wall**; you could also build a **Concrete-block wall** that is very durable and easy to paint. Whichever style you chose, use the right quantity of gravel and heavy stones: the heavier the stones, the stronger the wall!

<u>This are the essential materials you should have:</u>

- Retaining wall stones (bricks or stones)
- Gravel
- Shovel
- Paint or sticks
- Trowel
- Level
- Rake
- Plate compactor
- Landscape fabric (non-woven fabric)
- All necessary irrigation connections – *optional* - (tees, ells, sprinklers, heads, pipes…)
- Any electrical supplies you need – *optional* - (electric cables, pipes, junction boxes…)
- Builder's sand
- Compact hardcore for fundaments (mix of: 1 part of sand, 1 part of mortar and 1 part of gravel)
- Compact hardcore for bricks (mix of: 1 part of mortar and 1 part of gravel)

#Step 2: Dig the foundations

Remember: the first layer of bricks will be underground and not visible: it means you will not have to add it to your wall's height! Keep this in mind when you buy your stones because you will have to purchase 1-layer bricks more than all the others that compose the wall height on the whole. If you forget this, your budget plan could change due to the extra bricks cost or the additional delivery charge. When you measure the wall's high, you also must consider 1" distance from each stone, because you must add 1" about of mortar among the stones.

1. Dig a layer 10" deep below the ground level *plus the height of your bricks*, for all height of the tile you've bought (for example: if your

brick's height is 4", you will dig a 10+4" deep layer). Spread the soil using a rake

2. Put in the layer 10" deep of compact hardcore (mortar-sand-gravel); you should remain with only the size brick height.

#Step 3: Build your wall

1. When the layer will be solid, put a first layer of bricks. Each brick must be distance 1-inc about each other: put the first brick on the extremely left of the excavation, putting a bit of compact hardcore (mortar-gravel) below the bricks and along its sides, using a trowel. Take another brick and put a bit of compact hardcore under the brick and along its side. Repeat it until you have completed the first layer. Ensure the bricks are parallel on the ground using a level.

2. You should have covered all the ground-level; then, you can start with you first layer above the ground. Take another brick, put a bit of compact hardcore under the brick and along its side and place it on the left of the layer.

3. Repeat the step 4, up to your desired height. Try to cross the bricks with each other, as in the photo, to make the wall more resistant.

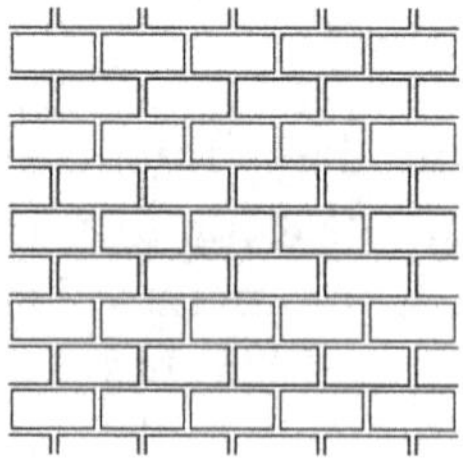

#Step 4: Enjoy your little wall!

1. Remove the residues from your wall, before they dry, using a cotton cloth wet.
2. Congratulations! You created your little wall!

Conclusion

A well-maintained landscape is a wonderful vision; this not only helps you to feel at home, it also offers compliments from family and friends. Landscapes enhance a person's way of living and to provide them with the utmost relaxation and comfort; it not only gives you a sense of wellbeing, but a well-maintained landscape also beautifies your residence's overall appearance. Creating a beautiful landscape in your garden is essential because it significantly contributes to your well-being and living conditions, and it provides a wider context to your lifestyle. People's feeling of well-being is enhanced by residing in aesthetically appealing landscapes that also provides them with a sense of spirituality. Most underdeveloped landscapes allow people to communicate with nature, revive their bodies and minds, and gain a greater appreciation for nature. Create your ideal landscape with the proper sets of principles, ideas, and inspiration you have gathered! Think about what extra entertainment you can add, which would not only suit your need but would provide your landscape with another level of excitement. For more practical experience, you can visit other people's houses.

Designing landscapes is all about one's personal desire and how effectively they put their art to practical use to create their ideal landscape. Landscaping really is a blast, and if you see it as a journey and a progression to work at until you reach the end, you really connect with it, and when you finish, it is that much more of an amazing experience! Keeping all of your maintenance at a small bite level will make it go fast and seem like a lot less work than if you wait and do it all at once. A little bit a day will go a surprisingly long way when you think about it; only spending a few minutes, a day on yardwork will greatly reduce the amount of time that you have to spend on it, and it will free up a lot more time to enjoy the yard that you have. So, you won't have to worry about sacrificing entire Saturdays to the job, because most of the work will already be done, and keeping it all under control will make it a lot easier to spend time with your friends or family have a barbeque! There is no reason why any one person should get stuck with all of the maintenance of the lawn!

So, what are you waiting for? You know what you need to do to start putting together your yard and how to make it into your own little paradise in this world! All you need to do now is get out there and do it, and you will see your new haven opening up before your very eyes.

Simply follow what you have learned in this book, and you are well on your way to developing a yard that you will want to spend hour after hour enjoying. Get your family involved in a fun and uplifting way, and you will be surprised at how much you can bond with each other when you are doing something as simple as lawn work; you could assign different jobs to different family members, together work on completing the jobs all at the same time, and in this way, everyone will feel important and involved. Always the time spends together is quality time and profitable. Kids' passion is great in the garden.

Set aside regular time to maintain the yard, but remember: **be sure to sit back and enjoy yourself when you are done!**

Thank you for reading. I wish you a happy life and a fantastic garden!

CPSIA information can be obtained
at www.ICGtesting.com
Printed in the USA
LVHW052243141220
674158LV00007B/84

9 781801 209342